The Northern Line

Origin, evolution and development of the most complex deep tube line

JONATHAN JAMES

KEY Books

TRANSPORT SYSTEMS SERIES, VOLUME 9

Front cover image: Trains of 1995 Stock pass at Finchley Central on 23 July 2022.

Title page image: A train of 1995 Stock arriving at High Barnet on 8 August 2021.

Contents page image: A train of 1995 Stock arriving in the new southbound platform at Bank on 15 October 2022.

Back cover image: The 1946 tube map included the planned Northern line extensions from Finsbury Park to Highgate and Alexandra Palace and between Mill Hill East, Edgware and Bushey Heath.

Acknowledgements

I would like to thank Tina Clarke and Malcolm Payne from the Transport for London Engineering Records Collection for their help and advice, and Malcolm Batten for providing some of the photographs. All photographs are by the author unless indicated otherwise.

I would also like to thank my wife Alison for her support. The book is dedicated to our youngest daughter Charlie, who sadly passed away, aged just 13, in December 2022. My royalties from this book will be donated to the Young Minds Trust.

I hope you enjoy the book and will see the Northern line in a new light when you next make a journey.

About the Author

Jonathan James has had a life-long interest in railways and has written more than a dozen books as well as numerous articles for a variety of transport magazines. His interest is wide-ranging and includes overseas railways, trams, underground railways, steam railways as well as narrow gauge and miniature railways.

He has worked in the railway industry since 1989 in a variety of different roles and is currently Head of Contract Management at MTR Elizabeth line. He is also a director of the Narrow Gauge Railway Society.

Published by Key Books
An imprint of Key Publishing Ltd
PO Box 100
Stamford
Lincs PE9 1XQ

www.keypublishing.com

The right of Jonathan James to be identified as the author of this book has been asserted in accordance with the Copyright, Designs and Patents Act 1988 Sections 77 and 78.

Copyright © Jonathan James, 2023

ISBN 978 1 80282 592 3

Typeset by SJmagic DESIGN SERVICES, India.

Contents

Introduction

I have always been interested in the Northern line and its history. One of my earliest memories is boarding a Northern line train at Morden, not far from where I grew up. The Northern line is undoubtably the most complicated of the deep-level tube lines, in terms of its operation and its history.

My purpose, in this book, is to explore the more unusual aspects of the line, including abandoned stations, uncompleted works, and proposed schemes. Back in the 1980s, I started researching the London Transport 1935–1940 New Works Programme, including the uncompleted Northern line extensions. I've also spent time at the Transport for London Engineering Records Collection, originally at West Kensington and more recently at Stratford, reviewing old drawings and plans.

The innovative City & South London Railway opened in 1890 and was the first deep-level underground electric railway in the world, following a last-minute decision to use electricity instead of cable haulage. The initial line between Stockwell and King William Street was a success and several extensions followed. The success of the City & South London Railway resulted in a plethora of new tube schemes being proposed, many of which were not progressed.

The Charing Cross, Euston and Hampstead Railway opened in 1907 between Charing Cross and Golders Green with a branch to Archway. The company was purchased by the American entrepreneur Charles Tyson Yerkes in 1900 and became part of his Underground Electric Railway Company (UERL). Further extensions followed to Embankment, Hendon and Edgware. The UERL purchased the City & South London Railway in 1913 and implemented a number of improvements. Between 1922 and 1924 a complicated project to enlarge the tunnels followed, all of which had been built to a smaller size than later tube lines.

The UERL was now in control of both the City & South London Railway and the Charing Cross, Euston and Hampstead Railway. Once the City & South London Railway tunnels had been reconstructed, attention turned to connecting the two railways. The City & South London Railway was extended from Euston to Camden Town in 1924. In 1926, the Charing Cross, Euston and Hampstead Railway was extended from Embankment to Kennington and at the same time the City & South London Railway was extended from Clapham Common to Morden.

A southbound train of 1996 Stock arriving at King's Cross St Pancras on 15 October 2022.

The UERL also purchased the District Railway, Baker Street and Waterloo Railway (later renamed the Bakerloo line) and the Great Northern, Piccadilly & Brompton Railway (later renamed the Piccadilly line).

In 1933 the London Passenger Transport Board was formed and took over responsibility for the Underground network, trams, buses and trolleybuses, and a number of private companies, including the UERL, were nationalised. This arrangement is largely in place today, with Transport for London controlling bus, tram, underground and some rail services in London.

Various names were used for the integrated railway before the Northern line was adopted in 1937.

The London Transport 1935–1940 New Works Programme, supported by government funding, proposed significant improvements to the transport network in London, including extensions to the Northern line. To facilitate this, the Northern City line between Moorgate and Finsbury Park was transferred from the Metropolitan line to the Northern line in 1939. The proposed extensions would have seen Northern line services taking over the former steam-worked branches from Finsbury Park to Alexandra Palace, High Barnet and Edgware via Mill Hill East. The Archway branch of the Northern line would have been extended to connect with the High Barnet branch at East Finchley, and at Edgware the Mill Hill branch would have been diverted to serve the underground station, with the old Edgware GNR station closed. A new extension would have been constructed from Edgware to Bushey Heath, which included a large new railway depot at Aldenham. World War Two disrupted the plans and the Northern line only reached High Barnet and Mill Hill East, with the lines between Finsbury Park and Alexandra Palace, and between Mill Hill East and Edgware, eventually closing. The part-built extension from Edgware to Bushey Heath was abandoned and the depot at Aldenham became a bus overhaul works.

The Northern City line was transferred to British Rail in 1975. Various improvements were progressed over the next few decades but it wasn't until 2021 that the line was extended again, with the opening of the Battersea Power Station extension.

* I have used lower case for Northern 'line' throughout the document for consistency and to align with current practice.

Jonathan James
Chatham, April 2023

The East Finchley archer, designed by sculptor Eric Aumonier, pointing towards London.

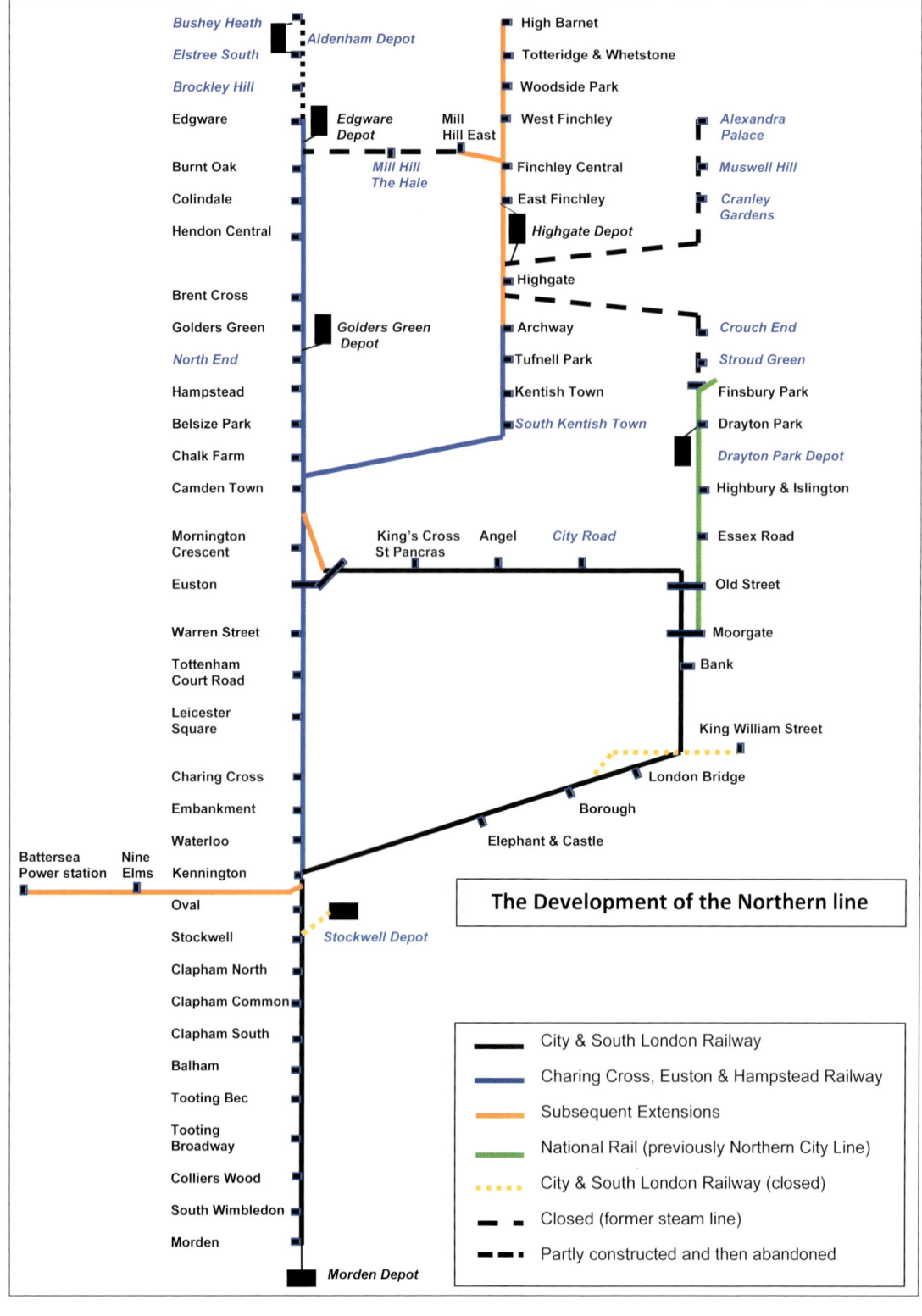

The Development of the Northern line

Legend:
- City & South London Railway
- Charing Cross, Euston & Hampstead Railway
- Subsequent Extensions
- National Rail (previously Northern City Line)
- City & South London Railway (closed)
- Closed (former steam line)
- Partly constructed and then abandoned

Chapter 1

The City & South London Railway

The first deep-level underground railway in London was the Tower Subway, which was a short cable-hauled line that crossed the River Thames near the Tower of London. The purpose was to provide an additional river crossing downstream from London Bridge. The 410m-line opened in August 1870 and closed in December of that year. The 2ft 6in-gauge carriage that ran on the line conveyed 12 passengers. Steam-powered lifts were provided at each end of the route to take passengers below ground and return them at the end of their journey. The railway was not economical to run and was converted to a foot tunnel, which customers paid to use. When Tower Bridge opened in 1894, which was free for pedestrians to use, the tunnel was closed.

The railway was constructed utilising a tunnelling shield originally conceived by Peter William Barlow and designed by James Henry Greathead. While the railway was not a success, the use of a tunnelling shield demonstrated that building deep-level underground railway tunnels in London was feasible.

Peter Barlow and James Henry Greathead proposed a new underground railway called the Southwark and City Subway, which received parliamentary approval in 1870. Unfortunately, funding was not secured, and the scheme did not progress. A number of other proposals followed, before the City & South London Railway was established. Initially called the City of London and Southwark Subway, the name was changed when authority was obtained to extend the railway beyond Elephant & Castle to Stockwell.

The first section of the City and South London Railway had six stations and ran between King William Street in the City of London and Stockwell via Borough, Elephant & Castle, Kennington, and The Oval (renamed Oval in 1894). Five of the six original stations form part of the Northern line today, although Stockwell has been resited and a number of the others have seen significant alterations. The official opening took place on 4 November 1890, with services to a fee-paying public commencing on 18 December 1890.

The railway was built to standard gauge (4 foot, 8½ inches) and was to be cable hauled, but during construction the decision was made to utilise electric traction instead. Trains were therefore designed to be powered by an offset centre 500V third rail (increased to 550V in 1915). The tunnels were constructed using cast iron rings with brick-lined tunnels in station areas.

The station at King William Street had a single track, with boarding and alighting platforms on each side, designed with cable haulage in mind. Stockwell had an island platform with crossovers just north of the station, along with a short locomotive siding and a steep ramp leading to the depot and power station. The depot and power station were located on the surface and were built on the former site of Spurgeon's Orphanage. Each station was equipped with two hydraulic lifts, although in 1897 a lift at Kennington was converted to electrical power, which proved successful and was used on future extensions.

There was a crossover linking the up-and-down lines at Elephant & Castle, which was also used for stabling trains. As is often the case on the London Underground network, the station platforms at Oval, Kennington, and Borough were at different levels, with the running tunnels often sitting above each other to minimise the land required. This resulted in the two running lines being reversed between Elephant & Castle and just outside King William Street. Sidings were later added at Stockwell and Kennington. All of the stations were fitted with hydraulic lifts and a spiral staircase. The original line had signal boxes at Stockwell, Elephant & Castle, and King William Street.

After leaving Borough, the line passed under the River Thames before approaching King William Street on a tight curve, which was also steeply graded. The single track at King William Street station, combined with the challenging approach, became a constraint. In 1895, King William Street's side platforms were replaced with an island platform with two tracks, increasing capacity on the route, although the tight curve and gradient

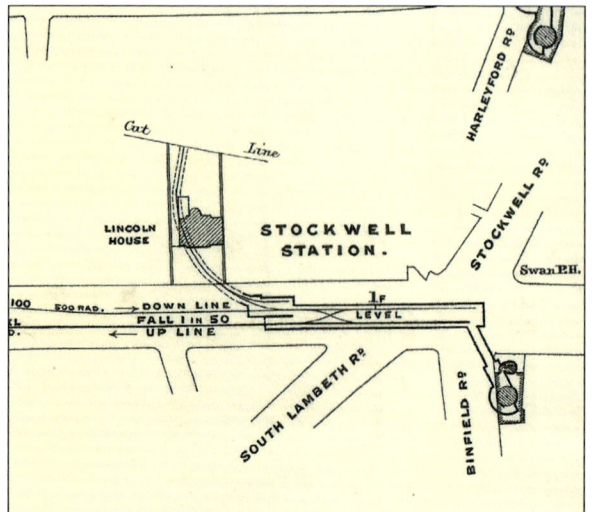
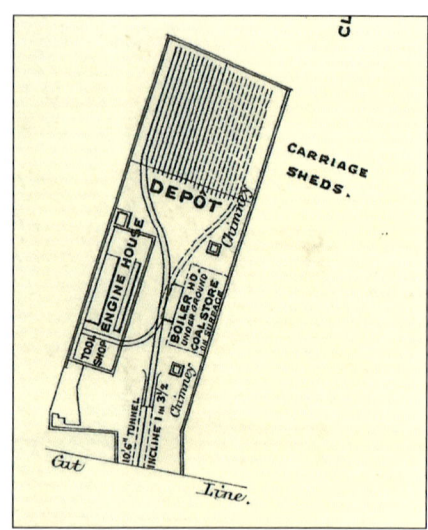

Above: These drawings show the original station at Stockwell including the ramp to Stockwell Depot, alongside Lincoln House, (left) and a simplified plan of Stockwell Depot (right). Additional sidings were later added at Stockwell station and at the depot. (Jonathan James collection)

Below: This plan shows an additional 'loop siding' (at centre top of the plan) that ran parallel with the southbound running line at Stockwell before connecting with the stabling sidings south of the station. On the top left is the spur to the depot, with the station on the right. The siding was later extended before being abandoned when the line was extended towards Clapham Common. (Copyright TfL from the TfL Engineering Records Collection)

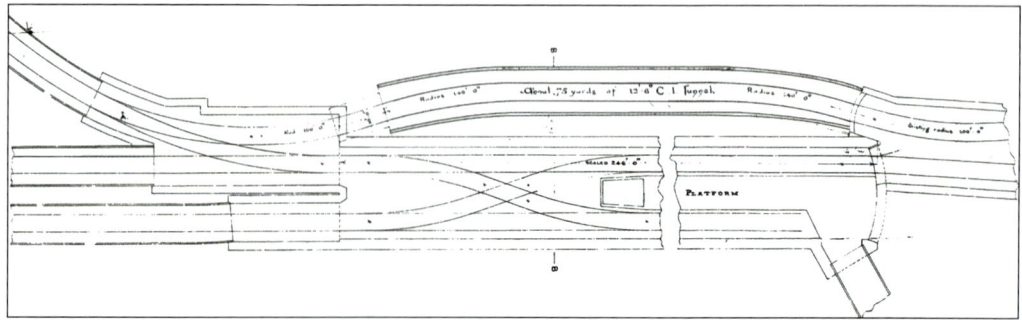

remained a challenge, and contributed to the station being closed a few years later. Trains were initially operated by one locomotive hauling three coaches.

In 1893, the southbound platform at Stockwell was extended in the Clapham direction, enabling two sidings to be provided. In 1895, another siding was added looping around the station and connecting with the sidings that were added in 1893. Stockwell Depot was also expanded with additional sidings.

The City & South London Railway was an immediate success and two extensions quickly followed, the first of which was to Moorgate Street (now Moorgate) to the north, which opened on 25 February 1900 and resulted in the closure of the spur to King William Street the previous evening. The extension included new stations at London Bridge and Bank (which replaced King William Street).

On 3 June 1900, a southern extension was opened from Stockwell to Clapham Common. Crossovers were provided at Clapham Common. Clapham Common and the other intermediate station at Clapham Road (now Clapham North) had narrow island platforms. In 1907, the steep ramp from Stockwell to the surface-level depot was replaced by a lift.

The City & South London Railway considered three options for a crossover road at Elephant & Castle. (Copyright TfL from the TfL Engineering Records Collection)

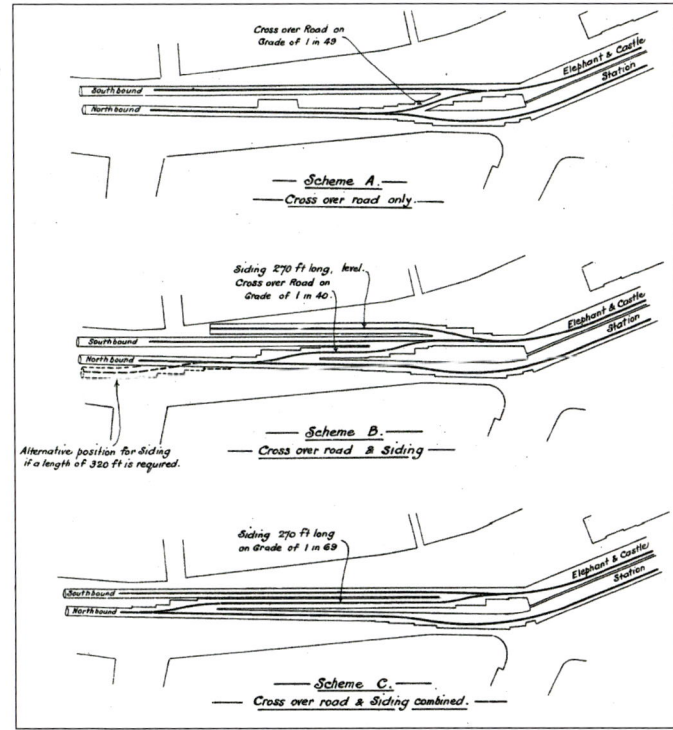

Scheme A.
Cross over road only.

Scheme B.
Cross over road & Siding

Scheme C.
Cross over road & Siding combined.

This drawing shows the final cross-over road at Elephant & Castle, which connected the up and down lines and also provided stabling for two trains. (Jonathan James collection)

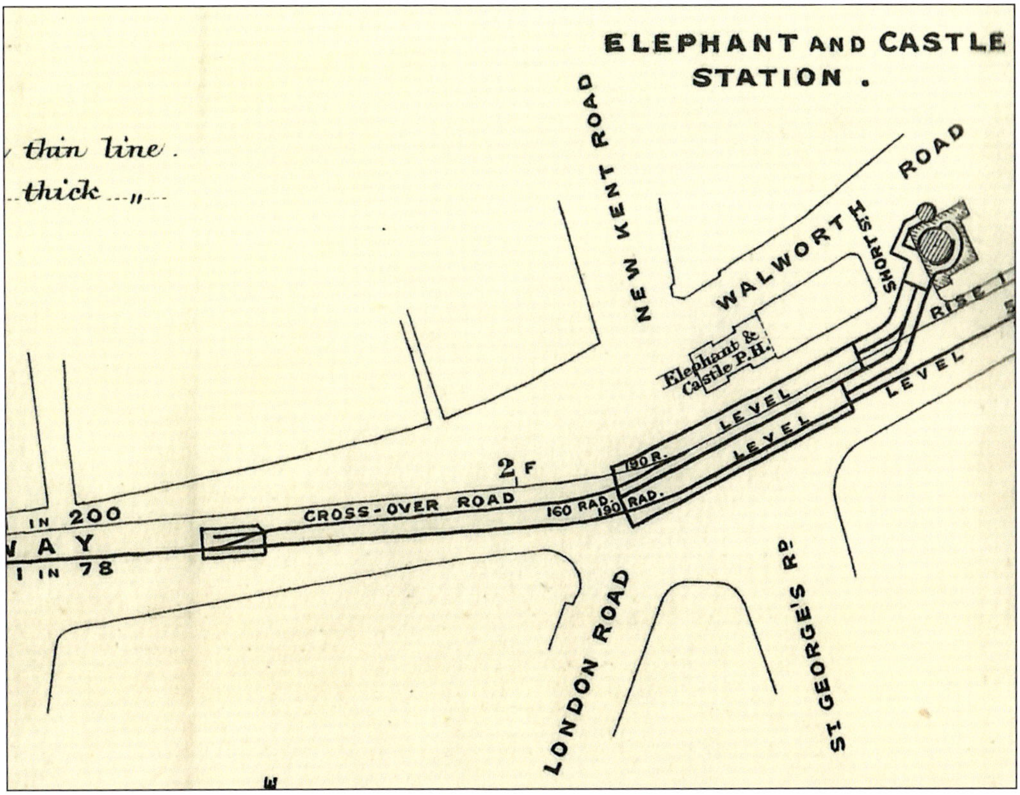

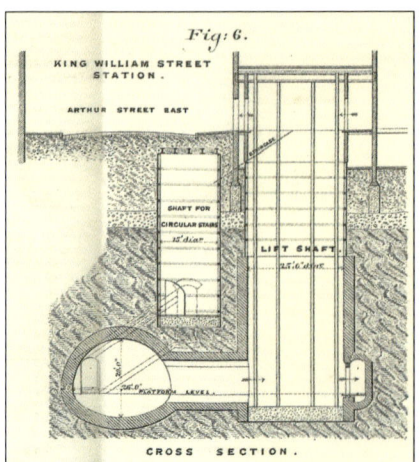
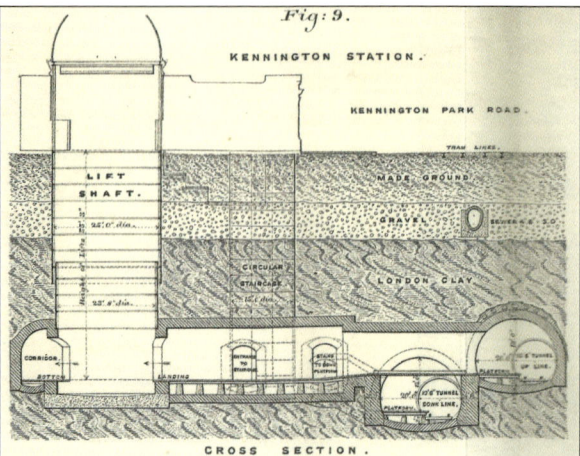

Above: **These drawings are of King William Street station (left) and Kennington station (right). The drawing of Kennington shows the platforms on two different levels. (Jonathan James collection)**

Below: **Moorgate Steet opened on 25 February 1900. This plan shows the two platforms, crossovers and short locomotive siding. The station opened with two lift shafts. (Copyright TfL from the TfL Engineering Records Collection)**

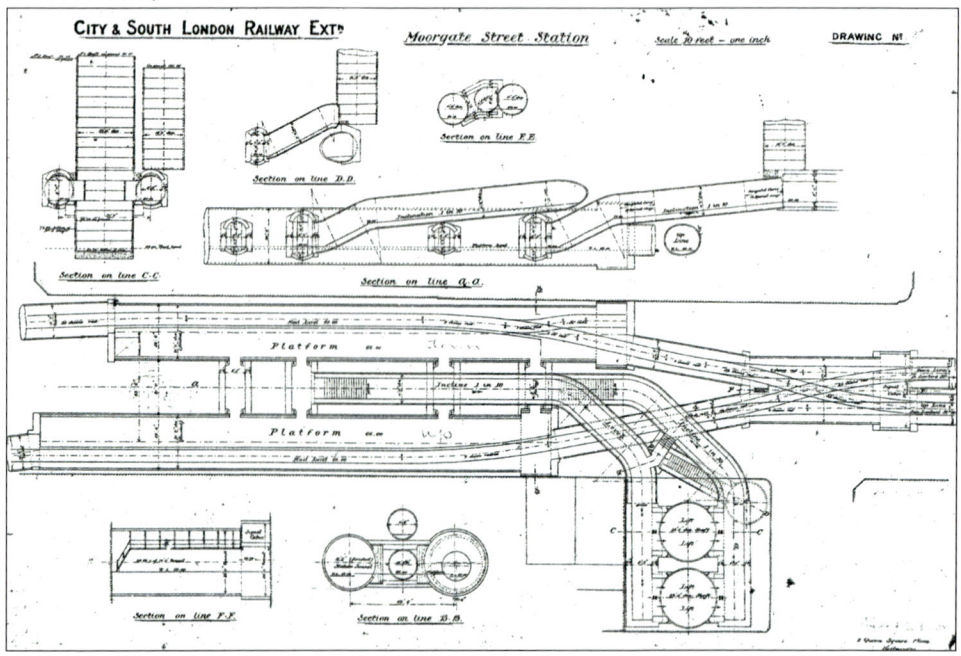

Longer trains were introduced to manage demand, and a further northern extension was opened from Moorgate Street to Angel in 1901, via Old Street and City Road. Angel had a crossover and several locomotive sidings. Initially trains were lengthened from three or four carriages in 1900, to five carriages in 1907, and to six carriages in 1923, although the platforms could only accommodate five-carriage trains, so passengers had to walk through the carriages to board and alight.

In 1907 the line was extended from Angel to Euston via King's Cross for St Pancras adding two more stations. Euston station had a traverser at one end of the platforms to move the locomotives, and a crossover and siding at the other end of the island platform. A signal cabin was provided at Weston Street between Angel and King's Cross for St Pancras, to increase capacity by splitting the signal section, which opened on 12 May 1907 and closed on 20 August 1921.

A number of sidings were provided along the route including at Clapham Common, Stockwell, Elephant & Castle, Bank, Moorgate Street, Old Street, Angel and Euston. London Bridge had a long trailing crossover siding, which could also be used to stable a train.

In 1913, the City & South London Railway was sold to the Underground Electric Railway Company (UERL), which quickly set about making improvements, including the introduction of non-stop trains (missing stations that were less busy such as at Clapham Road, Kennington, Borough and City Road). The power station at Stockwell closed in 1915, so power provision transferred to Lots Road power station in Chelsea.

Tunnel reconstruction

The City & South London Railway line tunnels had a smaller diameter than later tube lines. Between Bank and Elephant & Castle the tunnels had a diameter of 10ft 2in. From Elephant & Castle to Clapham Common, and between Moorgate Street and Euston, they had a 10ft 6in diameter. The tunnels between Bank and Moorgate Street were wider with an 11ft 6in diameter. Between 1922 and 1924 the original narrow tunnels were enlarged to accommodate larger rolling stock and enable integration with the Charing Cross, Euston and Hampstead Railway.

To accommodate the upgrade, Euston to Moorgate Street was closed from 9 August 1922 until 20 April 1924. Moorgate Street to Clapham Common was closed overnight from 9 August 1922 until 27 November 1923. Following a tunnel collapse at Elephant & Castle on 27 November 1923, this section closed from 28 November 1923 until 1 December 1924.

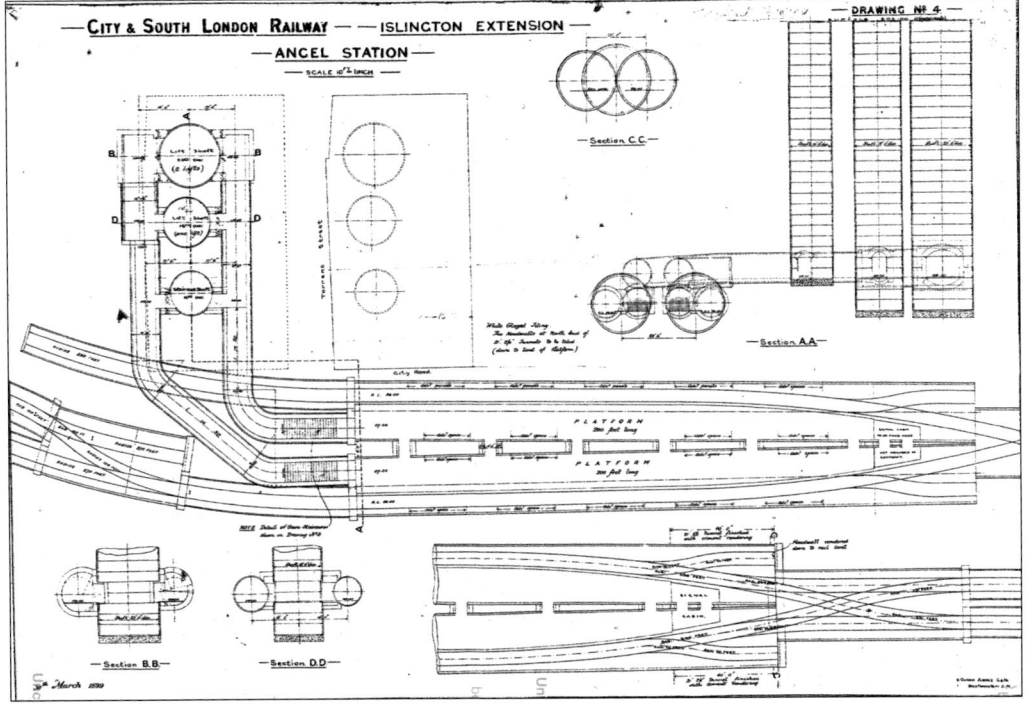

A plan of Angel station dated March 1899, showing the crossovers to the right of the drawing (inset bottom right) and the different locomotive sidings at both ends of the station. A signal box was located at the Moorgate end of the platforms. The passageways led to a staircase shaft and two lift shafts. (Copyright TfL from the TfL Engineering Records Collection)

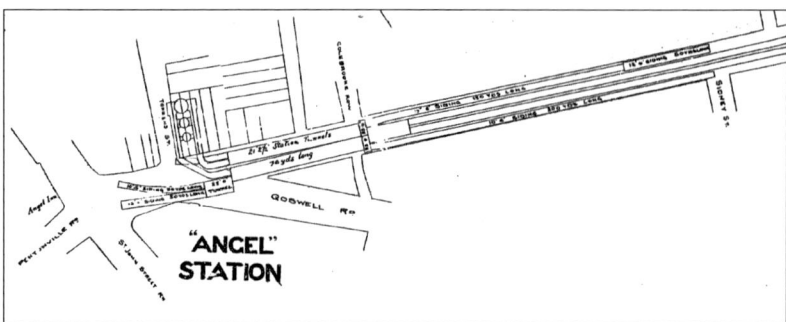

This slightly later plan showing two 200-yard sidings at the City Road end of Angel station. The northbound siding was retained until 1959. (Copyright TfL from the TfL Engineering Records Collection)

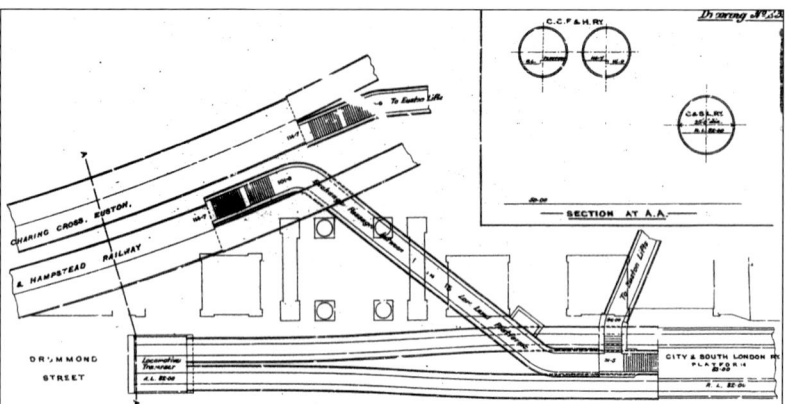

This drawing shows the original City & South London Railway station at Euston, including the locomotive traverser, along with the Charing Cross, Euston and Hampstead Railway platforms and the connecting subway. (Copyright TfL from the TfL Engineering Records Collection)

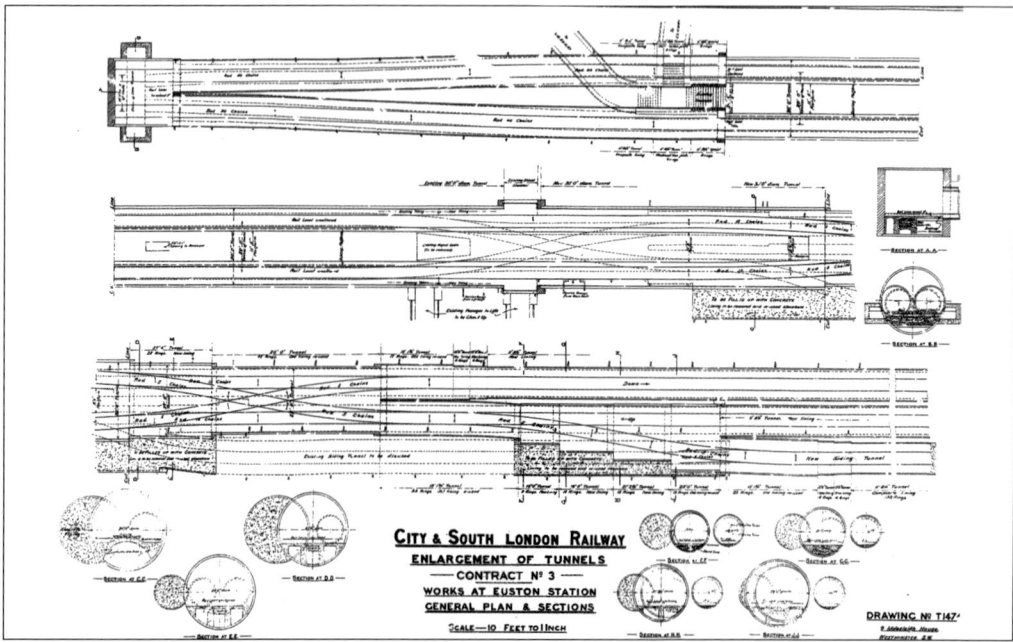

This drawing details arrangements for widening the tunnels at Euston and extending the island platform towards King's Cross for St Pancras. The site of the original crossovers and the revised location are shown, along with the original reversing siding and the new siding that was located further to the east, and which remained in use until the station was rebuilt for the Victoria line in 1967. (Copyright TfL from the TfL Engineering Records Collection)

The upgrade work included inserting additional tunnel segments; some sections of the line were realigned, including a long section near Elephant & Castle. Platforms were extended at the same time and a number of stations were modernised. During the rebuilding project, a siding was laid on the trackbed of the former King William Street branch.

A view of the City & South London Railway interior at Euston taken in 1908, showing the offset conductor rail and the narrow island platform that remained until the station was rebuilt ahead of the Victoria line opening. (Copyright TfL from the London Transport Museum Collection)

Above left: A memorial to James Henry Greathead 1844–96 located on King William Street. The text reads: J.H. Greathead, Chief Engineer, City and South London Railway, inventor of the travelling shield that made possible the cutting of the tunnels of London's deep level tube system.

Above right: The cable-operated Tower Subway preceded the City & South London Railway, but was only open for a few months. Not far from the Tower of London, one of the original entrances has been reconstructed, 17 April 2006.

Stockwell Depot closed in 1923 having been used as a staging point for the tunnel reconstruction works. It was used for a few more years by engineering trains before being completely closed around 1929. Stockwell station was rebuilt, slightly further south as part of the work and included the provision of a new siding. At Euston, the crossovers were moved towards King's Cross St Pancras and the original siding taken out of use. A new reversing siding was provided further east, which remained in use until 1967.

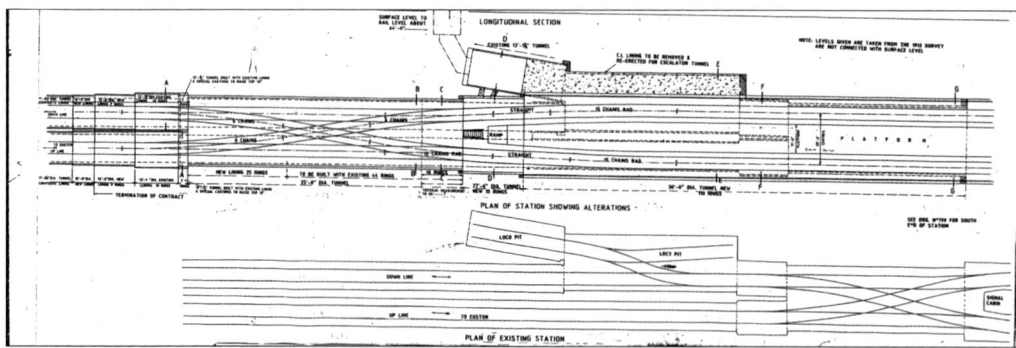

The drawing shows the original layout at Clapham Common (bottom) and the revised layout (top) following reconstruction as part of the tunnel-rebuilding scheme. The original layout included scissor crossovers and a short siding leading to two locomotive pits. The revised layout involved moving the crossovers further north, extending the island platform and removing the locomotive sidings. (Copyright TfL from the TfL Engineering Records Collection)

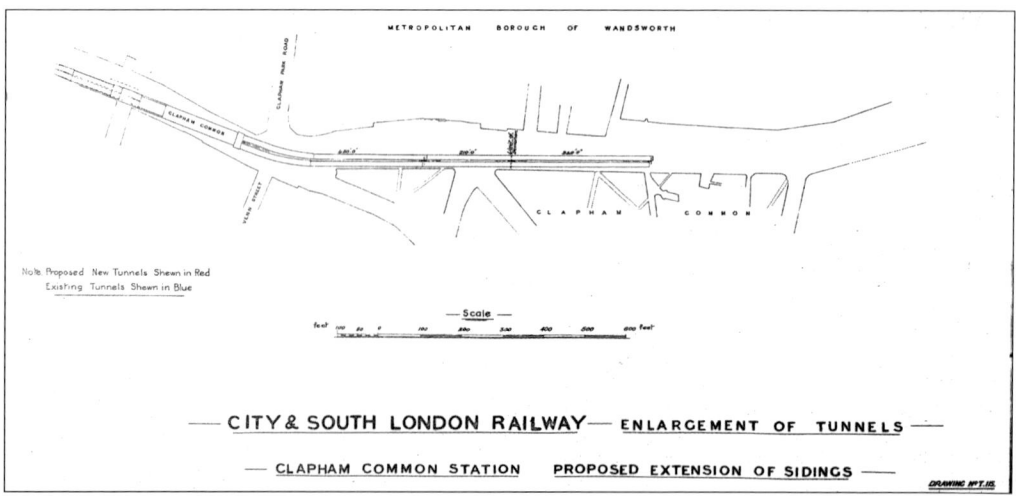

This plan, also produced for the tunnel enlargement project, shows the two stabling sidings that were constructed south of Clapham Common station, which were later used for the Morden extension. (Copyright TfL from the TfL Engineering Records Collection)

Chapter 2

The Charing Cross, Euston and Hampstead Railway

Originally called the Hampstead, St Pancras and Charing Cross Railway, this railway would originally have operated between Hampstead and Agar Street (near the Strand, and a short distance from Charing Cross) with a branch line to Euston and St Pancras. The main line would have run via Belsize Park, Chalk Farm, Camden Town and then via Tottenham Court Road and Oxford Street to Agar Street (for Charing Cross). Following a number of modifications, and a change of name, the Charing Cross, Euston and Hampstead Railway received parliamentary approval in 1893. The railway was built to standard gauge, but unlike the separate City & South London Railway, the tunnels were built to a larger size.

Subsequent changes were made to the route bringing the terminus closer to Charing Cross, with the station relocated from Agar Street to Craven Street and eventually to Villiers Street, on the opposite side of the main line station, which improved connections with the District Railway station at Charing Cross (now Embankment). The proposed branch line towards Euston and St Pancras was removed from the plans and instead the main route, which was originally going to follow Hampstead Road, was diverted eastwards to serve Euston station, before curving back to reach the original alignment near Mornington Crescent. The deviation removed the need for a junction and a terminus at St Pancras. A branch was also added from Camden Town to Kentish Town in 1899.

Funding issues prevented the scheme from progressing until the American financier Charles Tyson Yerkes purchased the company in 1900. He immediately proposed further changes to the scheme, adding an extension from Hampstead to Golders Green, and from Kentish Town to Highgate. An extension from Charing Cross to Victoria via Parliament Square was also proposed but this, along with the section between Archway and Highgate, was rejected.

At the same time a new company called the Edgware and Hampstead Railway was formed. This was quickly taken over by Charles Tyson Yerkes and his newly formed Underground Electric Railways Company (UERL). The scheme was modified to provide an end-on connection with the Charing Cross, Euston and Hampstead Railway at Golders Green.

Another railway to receive parliamentary approval was the Watford and Edgware Railway, which would have connected Watford to the Edgware and Hampstead Railway. The scheme did not progress and the Parliamentary Powers eventually fell away, although plans for an extension north of Edgware returned a couple of decades later.

Construction of the Charing Cross, Euston and Hampstead Railway eventually commenced in 1902 and the railway was ready to open in 1907, running from Charing Cross to Highgate (Archway) and to Hampstead and Golders Green where the depot was located. New stations opened at Leicester Square, Oxford Street (later renamed Tottenham Court Road), Euston Road (later renamed Warren Street), Euston, Mornington Crescent and Camden Town, where the routes diverged. The eastern branch had new stations at South Kentish Town (since closed), Kentish Town, Tufnell Park and Archway. The western branch had stations such as Chalk Farm, Belsize Park, Hampstead and Golders Green. Work also started on a station at North End, between Hampstead and Golders Green, but it was not completed. Power was supplied from Lots Road power station in Chelsea, which also provided electricity for the District Railway.

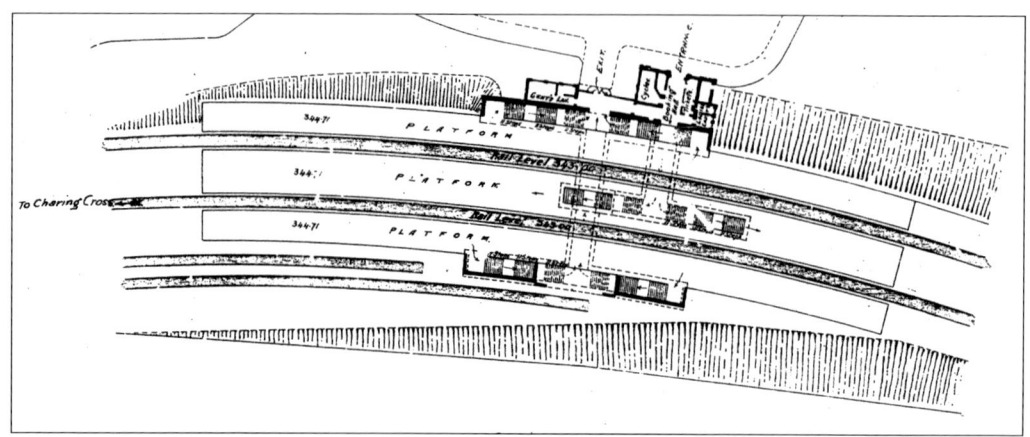

Golders Green originally had two tracks and four platforms. The outer platforms were used for arrivals, with the centre island platform used for departures. A third line was added on the depot side of the formation in preparation for the Hendon extension, creating two island platforms and a side platform adjacent to the Approach Road. (Copyright TfL from the TfL Engineering Records Collection)

At this time, the City & South London Railway and the Charing Cross, Euston and Hampstead Railway (also referred to as the 'Hampstead Tube') had separate stations at Euston. In 1914, both ticket offices were closed, but a subway was built connecting the two stations, and included an underground ticket office.

The original railway had scissor crossovers at Highgate (Archway), Golders Green and Charing Cross to enable trains to reverse into each platform with crossover lines at Hampstead and Mornington Crescent that could also be used to reverse trains. Signal boxes were provided at Charing Cross, Mornington Crescent, Camden Town, Hampstead, Golders Green and Highgate.

Fast trains were introduced at peak times from 1908, running non-stop between Highgate (now Archway) and Camden Town. Semi-fast services were also introduced missing Tufnell Park, Kentish Town or South Kentish Town. Limited-stop theatre trains commenced on the Golders Green branch in 1909, with daytime limited-stop trains introduced from 1913 to provide more attractive journey times.

In 1913, there was a proposal to connect the proposed Golders Green to Hendon extension with the Midland Railway at Hendon. The idea resurfaced in 1919 with proposals to run through-services to Harpenden, and again in 1923 when a more ambitious proposal would have seen trains travel through to Luton via St Albans. In 1919, proposals were made to extend the Highgate (Archway) branch to High Barnet and Alexandra Palace. This was not progressed, although that scheme also returned a few years later. There were further proposals in 1919, 1924 and 1933 to extend the Northern line from Archway to Highgate.

An extension from Charing Cross to Embankment opened in 1914 and consisted of a single-track loop, with a platform (the current northbound platform) providing a direct connection with the District Railway. Two sidings were originally proposed on the Embankment extension but were later removed from the scheme. The station opened as Charing Cross (Embankment) on 6 April 1914 but was renamed Charing Cross on 9 May 1915 and finally Embankment on 12 September 1976. The current Charing Cross station was renamed Charing Cross (Strand) on 6 April 1914 and then simply Strand from 9 May 1915, before receiving its current name in 1979 following reconstruction to accommodate the Jubilee line.

Chapter 3
Extensions and Integration

Euston to Camden Town

Following the acquisition of City & South London Railway by the Underground Electric Railway Company in 1913, which placed both railways under the same ownership, plans were drawn up to connect the City & South London Railway with the Charing Cross, Euston and Hampstead Railway by constructing a new tunnel between Euston and Camden Town. Work started in August 1922 and included the complicated remodelling of the junctions at Camden Town to connect the two railways and provide access to both the Edgware and Archway (Highgate) branches. The new connections opened on 20 April 1924, although trains on the City & South London Railway only travelled as far as Moorgate Street until 1 December 1924 as tunnel reconstruction work was still in progress.

Hendon and Edgware extension

The long-planned Hendon extension returned in 1921, drawing on government support to tackle high levels of unemployment, with work starting on the extension in 1922. The line from Golders Green to Brent (now Brent Cross) and Hendon Central opened on 19 November 1923. Scissor crossovers were provided at Hendon Central but were removed in 1926. The line was further extended to Edgware via Colindale and Burnt Oak, opening on 18 August 1924, although construction delays resulted in Burnt Oak opening on 27 October 1924. Space was provided for passing loops at Brent (now Brent Cross), which came into use in January 1925 for fast services, which ran non-stop between Edgware and Hendon Central or Golders Green. Some trains also skipped Mornington Crescent and Warren Street. Passive provision was also made for a third track between Hendon Central and Edgware. The loops at Brent were taken out of use on 23 August 1936. A turnback siding was also provided at Colindale, with signal boxes provided at Brent, Hendon Central and Colindale as well as at Edgware. A small depot and sidings were provided at Edgware, which originally opened with two platforms, a third being added on 20 November 1932.

Edgware to Watford

Planning authority to construct a railway between Watford and Edgware was in place from 11 August 1903, with most of the route protected from development, but the scheme did not progress. The UERL acquired the Watford to Edgware company in 1923. A 1923 report proposed an extension from Edgware to Watford via Bushey Heath and Bushey. In 1924, work was undertaken on the proposed northward extension to Watford, including land purchases. An extension from Edgware to Watford was once again considered in 1930 utilising the long-protected trackbed north of Edgware.

In 1931 there was a proposal to install stabling sidings north of Edgware on the route of the proposed Edgware and Watford Railway. In 1933 there were proposals for an extension from Edgware to Borehamwood East via the Moat Mount Estate, but priority was given to developing a route via Elstree to Bushey Heath instead. In 1934 there was a proposal to extend the Metropolitan line from Stanmore to Elstree, with a new depot at Aldenham. In 1935, there were proposals to construct a new line from either Stanmore or Edgware to Elstree, enabling trains to operate through to St Albans or Harpenden. In 1936, a similar scheme proposed a connection between the Northern line and the LMS at Mill Hill The Hale, enabling through trains to operate to St Albans, but neither scheme was progressed.

Charing Cross (Embankment) to Kennington and Morden

In 1922 plans were drawn up to extend the Charing Cross, Euston and Hampstead Railway from Embankment to Kennington via Waterloo to form a connection with the City & South London Railway. This involved rebuilding Kennington station with two more platforms and a reversing loop (to replace the loop at Embankment). A new reversing siding was also planned south of the station to enable trains on the City & South London Railway (via Bank) to terminate at Kennington as well.

At the same time, the City & South London Railway put forward plans to extend the line from Clapham Common to Morden and then on to Sutton via the Wimbledon to Sutton Railway, which was promoted by the Metropolitan District Railway and authorised in 1910. In addition, a complicated set of junctions would have been constructed south of Waterloo, which would have enabled Bakerloo line trains from Elephant & Castle to connect with the Charing Cross, Euston and Hampstead Railway (enabling direct trains from Elephant & Castle to Edgware and Highgate (Archway), and City & South London Railway trains from Sutton, Morden and Clapham Common to join the Bakerloo line (enabling direct services between south London and Watford Junction).

Another option considered was an extension of the Charing Cross, Euston and Hampstead Railway from Charing Cross (now Embankment) to Kennington, and then on to Streatham via Brixton. From Streatham the line would have continued to Sanderstead via Norbury, Thornton Heath and Croydon (probably using existing railway infrastructure). Following a number of objections, including from the Southern Railway, which operated the existing line, the scheme was simplified. The Bakerloo line connections were dropped as was the connection with the Wimbledon and Sutton Railway at Morden. The simplified project was authorised in 1923 with construction of the Clapham Common to Morden extension commencing on 31 December 1923. The Morden extension provided additional stations at Clapham South, Balham, Trinity Road (Tooting Bec), Tooting Broadway, Colliers Wood, South Wimbledon and Morden. The Embankment to Kennington via Waterloo section opened shortly afterwards in spring 1924. The work included construction of the loop at Kennington and a new depot at Morden.

The extension from Embankment (then called Charing Cross) to Kennington involved construction of a new southbound platform at Embankment. The original platform located on the former loop was retained as the new northbound platform. The new line from Embankment (then called Charing Cross) to Kennington opened on 13 September 1926 at the same time as the Morden extension.

Piccadilly line link

On 27 March 1927, a single-track connection between the Northern line and Piccadilly line was built at King's Cross to enable rolling stock to be transferred to and from Acton Works for overhaul. The link still connects the eastbound Piccadilly line with the northbound Northern line, and is usually referred to as the King's Cross loop.

The Northern line emerges

The Charing Cross, Euston and Hampstead Railway was sometimes referred to as the Edgware and Highgate Railway. The Hampstead & City line was used for a brief period after the City & South London Railway and the Charing Cross, Euston and Hampstead Railway were connected. From 1933, this was changed again to the Edgware, Highgate and Morden Line and then in 1934 to the Morden–Edgware Line before the Northern line was finally used from 28 August 1937.

The line now operated between Archway and Edgware to the north of London and Morden to the south of London with branches serving the City and West End of London.

Chapter 4
The Northern City Line

The Northern City line started life as the independent Great Northern and City Railway. The line opened on 14 February 1904 between Finsbury Park and Moorgate via Drayton Park, Highbury & Islington, Essex Road and Old Street and was built with main line-size tunnels, as it was intended that the Great Northern Railway would use the new railway to reach the City, relieving congestion at King's Cross. The two organisations failed to reach agreement on through-running arrangements and the Great Northern and City Railway was subsequently taken over by the Metropolitan Railway on 1 September 1913.

The railway was electrified between Finsbury Park and Moorgate from the start of operations, with two conductor rails on the outside of the running rails, and was underground with the exception of the station and depot at Drayton Park, which were on the surface.

A short extension from Moorgate to Lothbury (adjacent to the Bank of England) was planned, but other than a short section of tunnel at Moorgate, no work was undertaken. There were also proposals to connect the Great Northern and City Railway with the Metropolitan Railway near Moorgate. A separate proposal suggested a connection with the Waterloo and City Railway near Bank, but neither scheme was progressed.

As part of the 1935–1940 New Works Programme, plans were drawn up to integrate the Moorgate to Finsbury Park line with the Northern line, and provide through services between Moorgate and High Barnet/Alexandra Palace, in addition to peak-hour trains that would continue to shuttle between Moorgate and the existing low-level platforms at Finsbury Park. This would have involved a connection to the existing steam-worked lines to High Barnet and Alexandra Palace at Finsbury Park, including two new surface level platforms. From Finsbury Park, services would have called at Stroud Green, Crouch End, Highgate (where the existing station was rebuilt), Cranley Gardens, Muswell Hill and Alexandra Palace, and from Highgate to East Finchley, Finchley Central, West Finchley, Woodside Park, Totteridge and Whetstone and High Barnet. The old steam lines were to be electrified and a connection with the Archway branch of the Northern line would have been made at East Finchley. The side conductor rails were repositioned to the standard London Transport arrangement in May 1939 and the Metropolitan Railway rolling stock was replaced with standard stock. The line was then transferred from the Metropolitan line to the Northern line. Work also commenced on constructing new ramps to the high-level station at Finsbury Park, but only the southbound ramp was completed following the post-war abandonment of the Alexandra Palace electrification project.

Following the failed attempt to connect the Northern City line with Alexandra Palace and High Barnet as part of the 1935–1940 New Works Programme, the railway continued to operate as a shuttle service between Moorgate and Finsbury Park, and was referred to as the Northern City line. The small depot at Drayton Park remained open, with the standard stock being replaced by 1938 Stock in 1966. In 1960, there were plans to electrify the former steam route between Finsbury Park and Highgate, retained to facilitate rolling stock transfers between Drayton Park Depot and the Northern line at Highgate via Stroud Green and Crouch End, which were hauled by battery locomotives. In 1963, it was suggested that passenger services could be introduced on this route between Moorgate and East Finchley via Highgate, but this was not progressed.

There was a separate proposal to provide a connection with the Victoria line at Finsbury Park to enable Northern City line rolling stock to reach the Victoria line depot at Northumberland Park. This would avoid retaining the route between Finsbury Park and Highgate (Park Junction) via Stroud Green and Crouch End. On 3 October 1964, the line was closed between Drayton Park and Finsbury Park with the original Northern City line platforms at Finsbury Park being used for the southbound Victoria line and southbound Piccadilly line platforms (with the existing Piccadilly line platforms used for the northbound Piccadilly and Victoria lines). The redundant tunnels between Drayton Park and Finsbury Park were blocked.

A new northbound tunnel and platform were constructed at Highbury and Islington to provide a cross-platform interchange with the Victoria line. In the southbound direction, the former Northern City line northbound platform was used by the southbound Victoria line while the southbound Northern City line platform was retained.

Consideration had been given to diverting the Northern City line to new surface platforms at Finsbury Park, utilising the connections built for the 1935–1940 New Works Programme, but in the event the service was cut back to Drayton Park. Consideration was also given to reducing the service to run between Moorgate and Highbury & Islington only. The truncated Moorgate to Drayton Park section continued to operate as a shuttle, but despite the new Victoria line interchange at Highbury & Islington, traffic numbers were subdued.

The original 1904 concept returned in the mid-1970s, when the decision was made to finally connect the Northern City line with the main line railway network at Finsbury Park. The section between Moorgate and Old Street closed on 6 September 1975, with the remainder of the route closed on 4 October 1975. The line was transferred from London Transport to British Rail the following day, enabling works to commence to convert the line for mainline operation. The British Rail 'Great Northern Electrics' service commenced in August 1976 between Moorgate, Finsbury Park and Hertford North/Welwyn Garden City.

Until 1970, rolling stock transfers were hauled by battery locomotive from Drayton Park to Park Junction via Crouch End and Highgate. Due to a weak bridge at Crouch End, single-line working was put in place between 1967 and 1970. The weak bridge eventually led to the line being closed in 1970, with the flyover at Finsbury Park demolished in 1972. From 1970, until the line was handed to British Rail in 1975, rolling stock was transferred via King's Cross and the Metropolitan Widened Lines in order to reach the underground network and then onwards to Golders Green or Acton Works.

A 1938 Stock unit standing at Drayton Park on 26 September 1975, shortly before the route was transferred to British Rail. At this point the line was operating as a shuttle service between Drayton Park and Old Street (Malcom Batten).

313048 arriving at Drayton Park with a train for Moorgate on 1 July 2017, utilising a connection built as part of the 1935–1940 New Works Programme, which would have seen through-trains from Moorgate to High Barnet and Alexandra Palace via Finsbury Park. This rolling stock has since been replaced by Class 717 EMUs. Trains switch from overhead AC to third-rail DC traction at Drayton Park station.

The Great Northern and City Railway opened in 1904. The company received consent for a short extension from Moorgate to Lothbury (near the Bank of England) in August 1902, but only a short section of tunnel was constructed. The Greathead tunnel shield is still in place at the far end of the tunnel. The company was taken over by the Metropolitan Railway in 1913, before becoming part of the Northern Line in 1939. The route was transferred to British Rail in October 1975.

Chapter 5
Uncompleted Plans

Proposed extensions to Sutton, North Cheam, Epsom and Morden Park

The line between Wimbledon and Sutton via St Helier was originally promoted by the Metropolitan District Railway and was authorised in 1910. Some alterations were carried out at Wimbledon station in 1913 to facilitate the extension but otherwise little progress was made, although the line appeared on some underground maps in 1923.

- The City & South London Railway proposed a junction with the Wimbledon to Sutton line at South Morden, which would have enabled both District Railway and City & South London Railway services to reach Sutton. The depot at Morden would have been shared by the Metropolitan District Railway and the City & South London Railway.
- In 1919, Frank Pick, the commercial manager at the UERL, produced a report proposing various new railway extensions, including an extension of the City & South London Railway from Clapham Common to Tooting Broadway, Tooting Junction, Mitcham and Carshalton, but the scheme was not progressed.
- The 1923 proposals would have seen stations at Nightingale Lane, Balham, Tooting Bec, Tooting Broadway, Merton Grove, North Morden, South Morden, Sutton Common, Cheam and Sutton. The Southern Railway objected, but a compromise was eventually reached, which enabled the City & South London Railway to reach Morden. The Southern Railway constructed the line between Wimbledon and Sutton (often referred to as the Wimbledon Loop), which opened between Wimbledon and South Merton on 7 July 1929, and to Sutton on 5 January 1930 (the line is now served by Thameslink services).

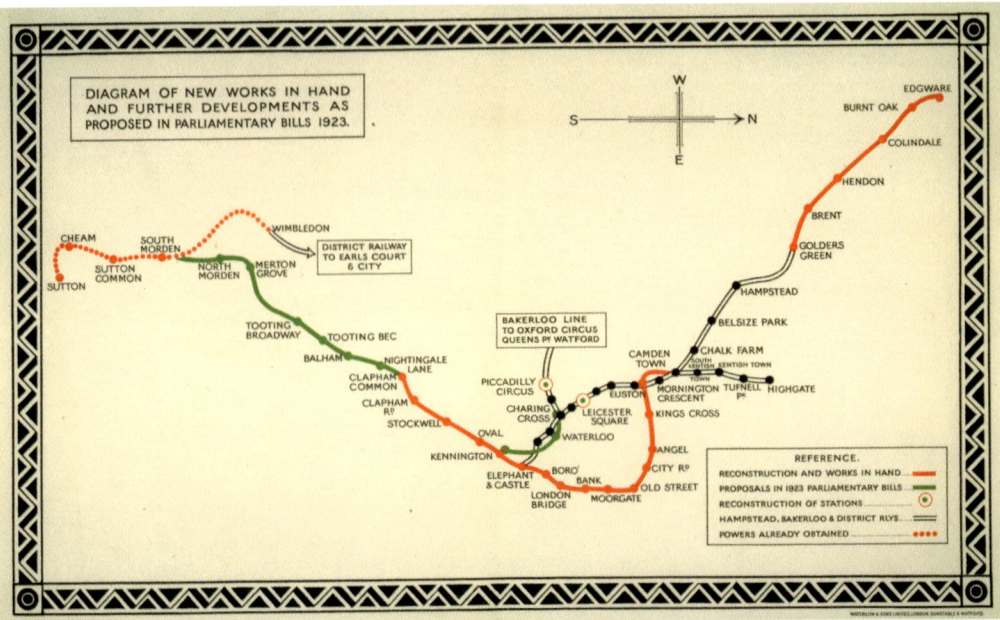

This map, dated December 1922, shows details of the proposed railway schemes, which would have included an extension to the City & South London Railway to Sutton, sharing tracks with the District Railway between South Morden and Sutton. The Bakerloo line would also have been connected with the Northern line.
(Copyright TfL from the London Transport Museum Collection)

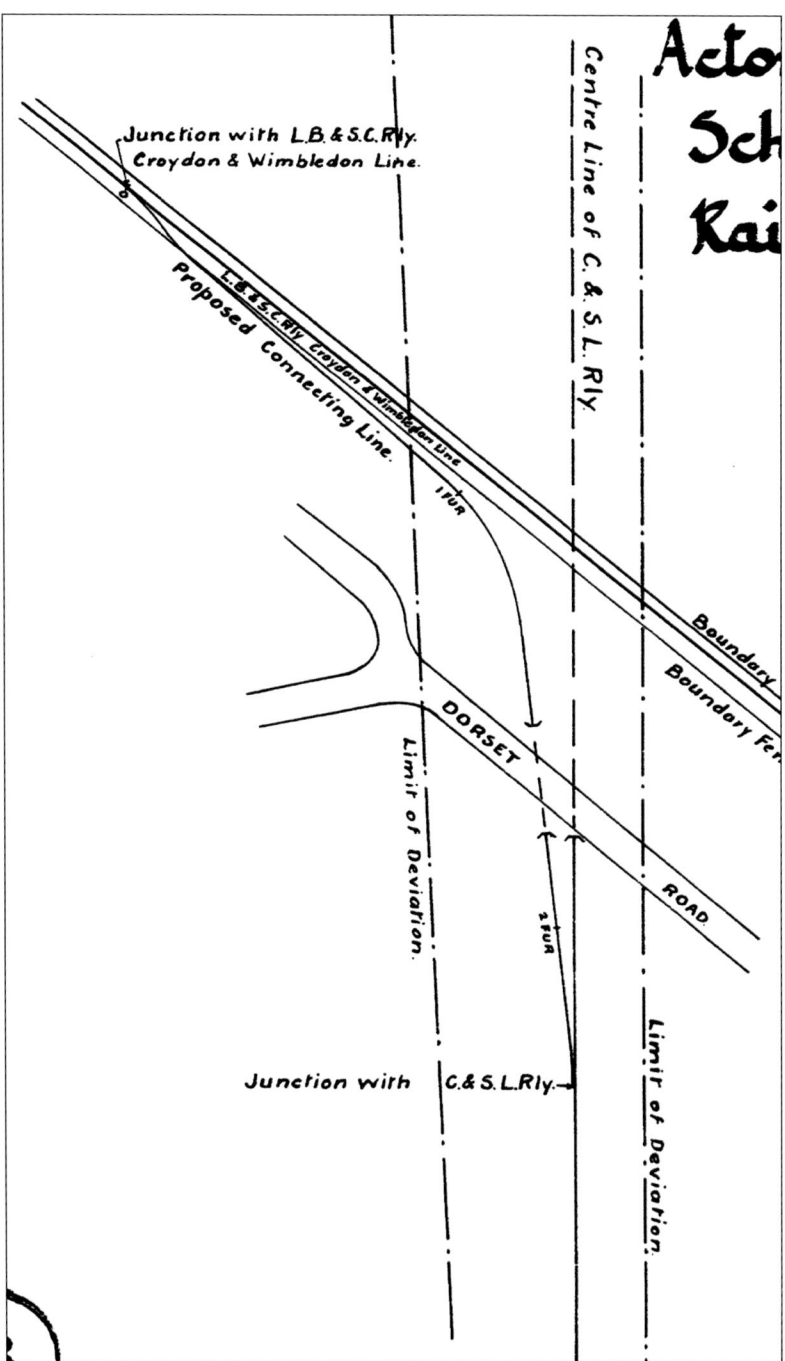

This plan is dated 16 January 1924 and shows details of a proposed link between the City & South London Railway and the London Brighton & South Coast Railway (Croydon and Wimbledon line) between Morden and South Wimbledon stations. The drawing is titled: *'Connection between Hampstead Group of Railways and Acton Works. Plan showing proposed connecting link Scheme D at Morden C & SLR to Southern Railway'*. The Southern Railway connection would have been between the modern day Morden Road and Merton Park tram stops, facing the Wimbledon direction. The link would have been used for rolling stock transfers only (Copyright TfL from the TfL Engineering Records Collection).

The London and Home Counties Advisory Committee produced a report in 1936–37 that recommended an extension of the Northern line from Morden to Epsom, the introduction of longer trains, or provision of express tunnels between Morden and Kennington. Land was identified for a station at North Cheam but the Granada cinema was subsequently built on the site. A further study suggested building express lines between Morden and Clapham Common, which would then have continued to Victoria. These schemes did not progress on cost grounds.

In 1938, the London Passenger Transport Board drew up plans for a short extension from Morden to Morden Park, providing an interchange with Morden South station on the Wimbledon to Sutton Line. Four options were considered:

Scheme A, Option One – Scheme A was developed in more detail and would have seen a twin-track extension from Morden to Morden Park, where a new station would have been built on playing fields opposite Morden South station. The station would have consisted of a 500ft-long island platform, with provision for a future extension of the line towards North Cheam and Epsom. The northbound line would have branched off immediately after the London Road bridge at Morden, before skirting the southwest side of Morden depot and passing under the Southern Railway embankment to reach the new station. The southbound line would also have left the depot access tracks just south of the London Road bridge but would have entered a single bore tunnel that would have passed beneath the depot and Southern Railway embankment before joining the northbound line at a pair of scissor crossovers just outside the new station at Morden Park.

Scheme A, Option Two – A variation to Scheme A, Option One above showed both tracks running in a tunnel between London Road and the new station at Morden Park, passing beneath the depot and Southern Railway embankment.

Scheme B – This would have consisted of a single-track loop around the depot, with a platform near Morden South station.

Scheme C – This option would have seen a single-track extension from the northbound track between Morden and Morden Depot, branching off just beyond the London Road bridge and continuing to a single platform at Morden Park alongside the depot building (for further details see the *London Railway Record* Number 25, October 2000).

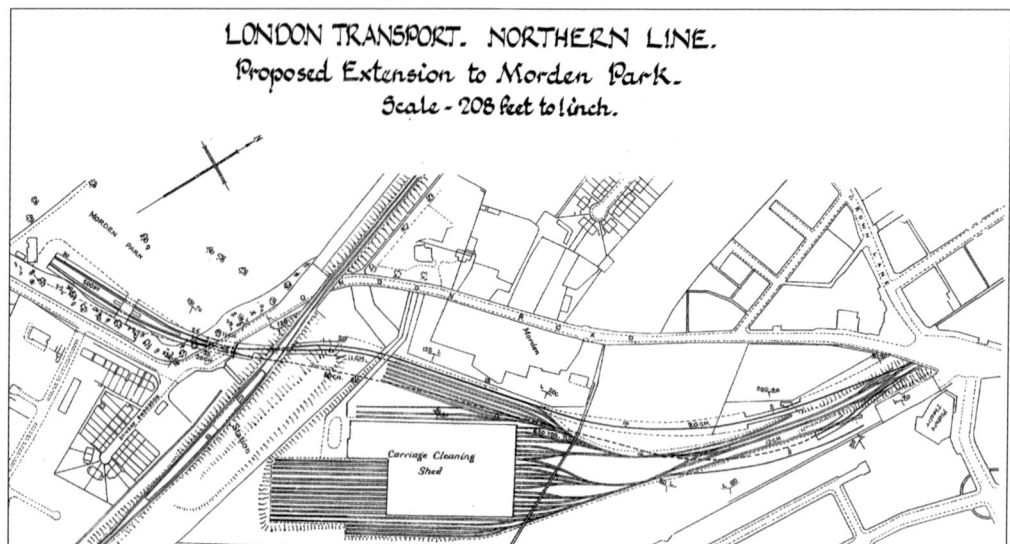

Scheme A, Option One, showing the proposed new station at Morden Park on the left, with Morden Depot in the centre of the plan, and the route towards Morden station to the right. (Copyright TfL from the TfL Engineering Records Collection)

This view is looking towards Morden, with the Wimbledon to Sutton railway crossing on the bridge. Under Scheme A, Morden Park station would have been on the playing fields to the left of this view, which was taken on 22 April 2000.

Scheme C would have been a simpler proposition, with a single platform adjacent to the depot building within walking distance of Morden South station. This plan shows the route between Morden station (left) and the single platform at Morden Park (bottom right). (Copyright TfL from the TfL Engineering Records Collection)

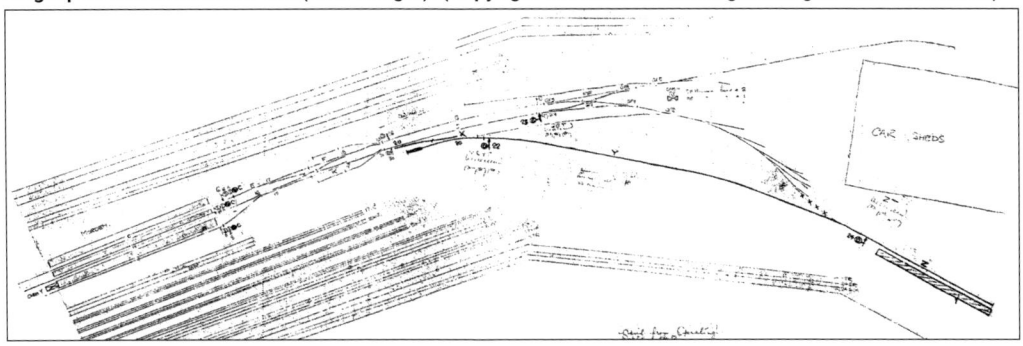

The London Transport 1935–1940 New Works Programme

Designed to stimulate economic growth as well as deliver significant improvements to the London transport network, the 1935–1940 London Transport New Works Programme identified eight separate schemes, listed A to I, which included main line electrification between Fenchurch Street/Liverpool Street and Shenfield; extensions to the Central line to the east and west of London; improvements to the Bakerloo and Metropolitan lines; rebuilding of a number of busy underground stations; along with the conversion of trams to trolleybuses. The total pre-war cost of the works was £44,777,000. Schemes C, F and H were relevant to the Northern line.

Scheme C – North London, involved the Northern line and was costed at £6,731,000 in pre-war prices. The works were to be jointly delivered by the London & North Eastern Railway (LNER) and the London Passenger Transport Board (LPTB) including the cost of additional rolling stock.

Scheme C	
(1)	Electrification of LNER branch lines from Finsbury Park to Alexandra Palace, High Barnet and Edgware, and doubling of Edgware branch, including improvements to stations, resignalling etc, but excluding rolling stock.
(2)	Construction and electrification of connecting lines between LPTB Northern City line and LNER branch lines covered by item (1) through Finsbury Park Station (LNER).
(3)	Resignalling of Northern City line, altering platforms to tube train height, and installation of standard current rails.
(4)	Extension of Highgate branch of LPTB Northern line to East Finchley (LNER) with interchange station for Alexandra Palace branch at Highgate station (LNER), together with new tracks, sidings and station at Edgware, excluding rolling stock.
(5)	Rolling stock for items (1), (2), (4) and (7).
(6)	Improvements to existing Northern line Camden Town substation.
(7)	Elstree extension, excluding rolling stock, but including a new depot at Bushey Heath.

Scheme F also included reconstruction of underground stations at King's Cross and Tottenham Court Road. Enhancements to the power supply, including work at Lots Road and Greenwich power stations, was proposed under **Scheme H**. Work on the extensions commenced in November 1936 with all works expected to be completed by December 1940.

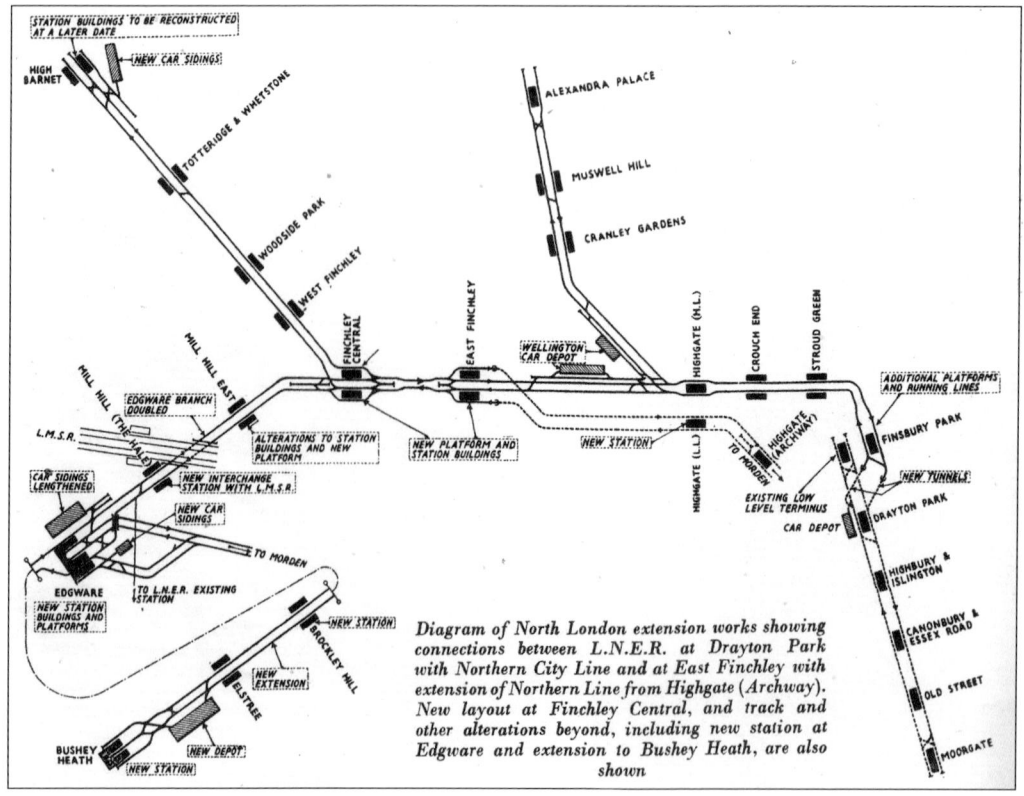

Diagram of North London extension works showing connections between L.N.E.R. at Drayton Park with Northern City Line and at East Finchley with extension of Northern Line from Highgate (Archway). New layout at Finchley Central, and track and other alterations beyond, including new station at Edgware and extension to Bushey Heath, are also shown

A diagram of the proposed works (reproduced with permission from Improving London's Transport published by the *Railway Gazette* in May 1946).

Proposed station sites

A number of additional station sites were considered but not progressed, including:

Deans Lane/Deansbrook Lane, between Mill Hill East and Edgware.
Finchley Manor, between East Finchley and Finchley Central.
Watford Way/Copthall, Between Mill Hill East and Mill Hill The Hale.
Willenhall Park/Barnet Vale, between Totteridge & Whetstone and High Barnet.

Proposed train services

The Northern line train service would have been very complicated. The standard train service pattern over the new extensions would have been as follows:

Moorgate–Alexandra Palace/High Barnet (peak)/East Finchley (off-peak).
Moorgate–Finsbury Park (low level) (peak).
Bushey Heath via Mill Hill East, Highgate and Charing Cross.
High Barnet via Highgate and Charing Cross.
Finchley Central via Highgate and Bank.

Both East Finchley and Finchley Central would have been used for reversing trains. Services on the Bushey Heath extension would have operated via Mill Hill East, Highgate and the Charing Cross branch. Cross platform interchange would have been provided at Edgware to enable passengers to and from Bushey Heath to connect with services via Golders Green.

Archway to Edgware, High Barnet and Mill Hill East

The line was designed to enable nine-carriage trains to be introduced at a later date, although not all of the enabling work was completed. Highgate station was renamed Archway (Highgate) on 11 June 1939, then simply Archway in 1947. One of the two sidings beyond Archway (Highgate) became the new northbound line, while the other became a centre-reversing siding, with a new southbound line constructed.

The first section to open was between Archway (Highgate) and East Finchley on 3 July 1939, although the new interchange station at Highgate did not open until 19 January 1941. Some of the station works at Highgate

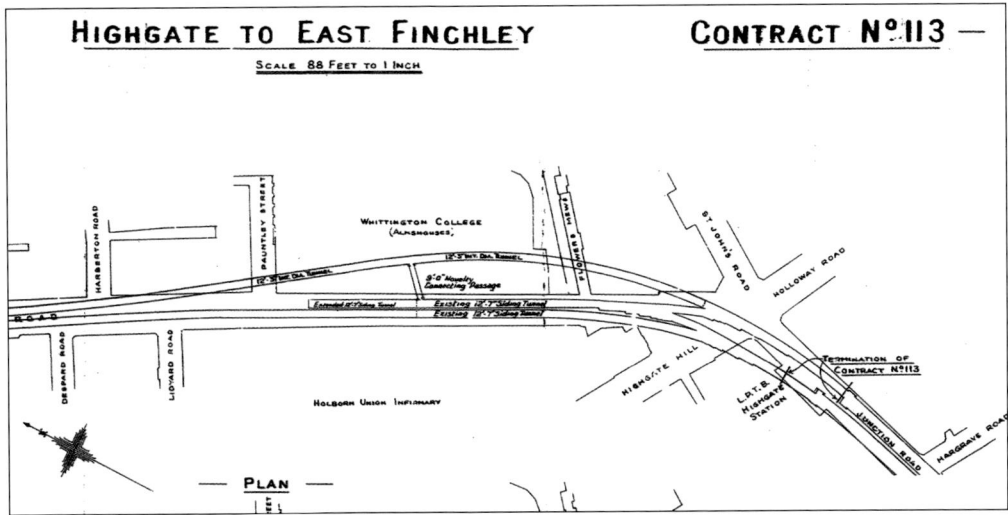

This plan, dated 2 November 1936, shows the new southbound line between Highgate and Archway as well as the two original sidings at Highgate (Archway), one of which has been extended to form the new northbound line towards East Finchley. (Copyright TfL from the TfL Engineering Records Collection)

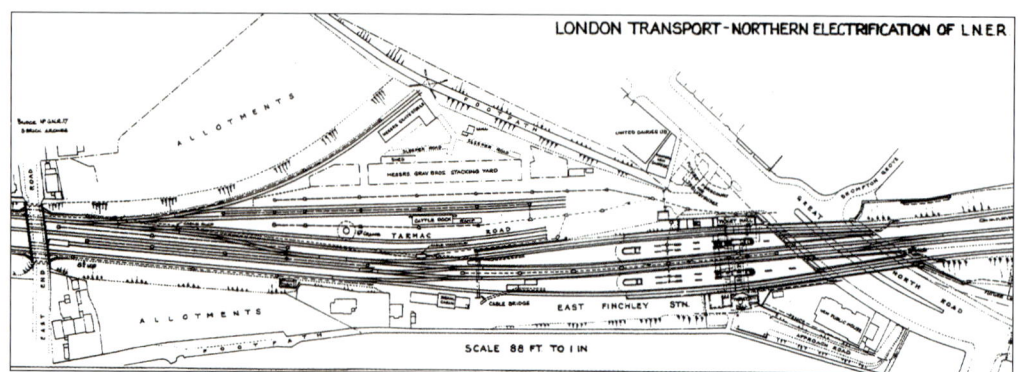

This plan shows East Finchley station, which was rebuilt with four platforms as part of the 1935–1940 New Works Programme. The outer platforms would have been used by trains to and from Archway, while the central platforms would have been used by services to and from Moorgate via Finsbury Park. The centre platforms are still in use today by empty trains to and from Highgate Depot. A turnback siding was provided at the Finchley Central end of the station. (Copyright TfL from the TfL Engineering Records Collection)

A train of 1959 Stock was painted in heritage livery in July 1990 and is seen here in Platform 2 at East Finchley on 15 December 1991 (Malcolm Batten).

were never completed, including a statue of Dick Wittington that would have been placed above the entrance on Archway Road near the Woodman pub. At ground level, a new high-level station was built on the site of the original GNR station.

East Finchley station was rebuilt with four platforms, together with a reversing siding north of the station. The line between East Finchley and Park Junction was also electrified, although the central platforms at East Finchley were not completed straightaway. These provided access to Highgate Depot (previously called Wellington Sidings) and Highgate Wood Sidings, which provided additional stabling.

Steam services continued to operate between Finsbury Park, Alexandra Palace, High Barnet and Edgware (LNER station) while the works were undertaken, including freight services to a number of the stations that retained a goods yard.

Steam services on the Alexandra Palace branch continued to call at the rebuilt Highgate high-level platforms, which were fitted with London Transport 'bullseye' signs, until services were withdrawn in 1954.

Finchley Church End was renamed Finchley Central, although the proposed station reconstruction was not progressed. The new station would have had four platforms, replacing the current station, which still has three platforms. Reversing sidings were provided at each side of Finchley Central.

The line between Finchley Church End (later renamed Finchley Central) and Edgware usually operated as a shuttle service in steam days. The single line was due to be doubled as part of the 1935–1940 New Works Programme, but priority was given to completing the High Barnet branch. However, a single track was electrified as far as Mill Hill East and opened on 18 May 1941, mainly to serve Mill Hill barracks. The second platform at Mill Hill East was not constructed and services used the existing single platform, which was not rebuilt. The Dollis Brook viaduct between Finchley Central and Mill Hill East was originally constructed to accommodate double-track.

Northern line services were extended from East Finchley to High Barnet via Finchley Central, West Finchley, Woodside Park and Totteridge & Whetstone on 14 April 1940. Eight sidings were provided at High Barnet, including provision for a second shunt neck if required at a later date.

High Barnet

In 1935–36 London Transport investigated extending the Northern line from High Barnet to a new station closer to the town centre at either Barnet Church or Chipping Barnet, but the proposal was not progressed.

A new station building was proposed at High Barnet as part of the 1935–1940 New Works Programme, which would have facilitated a northern extension, but the work was deferred. In 1963–64 there was another plan to rebuild High Barnet station, including a large car park above the new station, but the scheme was not progressed.

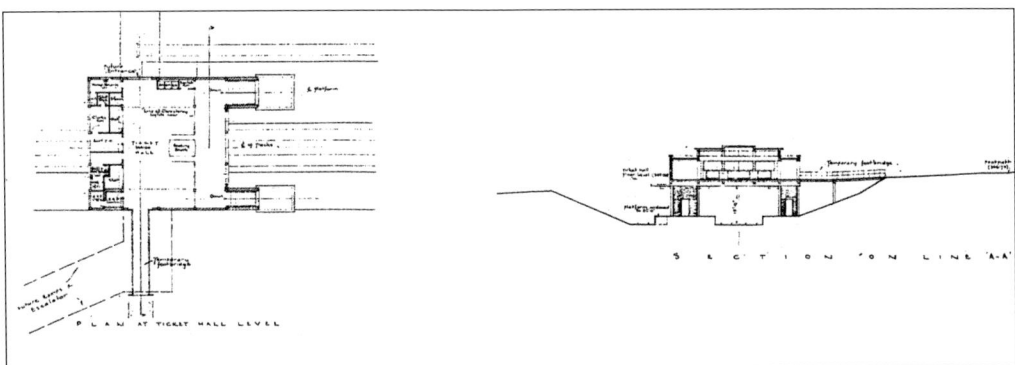

This drawing shows the new station building proposed at High Barnet as part of the 1935–1940 New Works Programme. This was a lower priority scheme and the proposed rebuilding did not take place. (Copyright TfL from the TfL Engineering Records Collection)

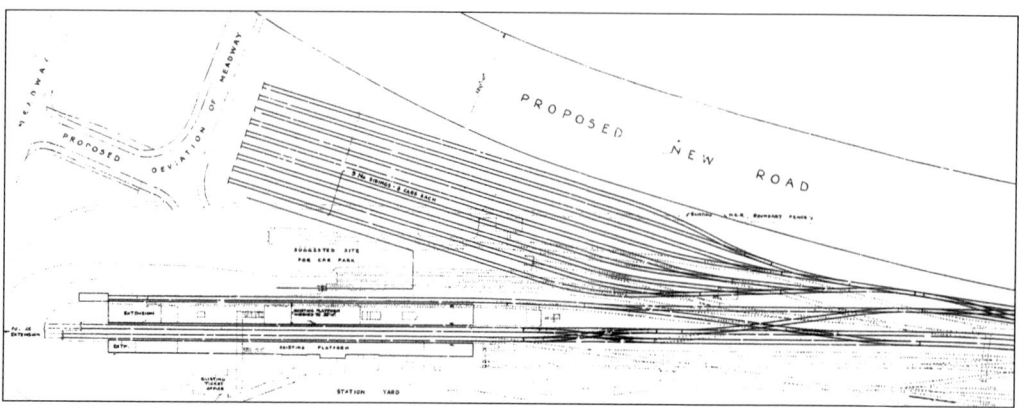

The plans for High Barnet included an extension of the existing platforms and the provision of nine new sidings. A new station building was also proposed, but was not progressed. (Copyright TfL from the TfL Engineering Records Collection)

The Northern City line

The Northern City line conductor rails were originally positioned at each side of the running rails, but were altered to the usual London Transport third and fourth rail position in May 1939. The plan was to operate through-trains from Moorgate to Alexandra Palace and High Barnet via new high-level platforms at Finsbury Park, with a peak hour shuttle between Moorgate and existing Finsbury Park (low level) platforms. The depot at Drayton Park was to be modernised and retained.

Alexandra Palace to Drayton Park

The connection to the Northern City line at Drayton Park was completed in the southbound direction, but only partly completed in the northbound direction. The southbound line was later connected to Highbury Vale yard to enable rolling stock transfers to take place. The northbound connection was completed when the route transferred to British Rail in 1976.

The steelwork was erected for the new high-level island platforms at Finsbury Park, although the work was not completed. From Finsbury Park, the existing route to Alexandra Palace/East Finchley was to be upgraded. Cable routes and conductor rails were installed along most of the route and a conductor rail and a new substation were built at Crouch Hill and Muswell Hill. The platforms at Crouch End station were also modified and the new high-level station at Highgate was constructed.

Steam operated passenger and freight services continued to travel over the route after work was suspended, until the withdrawal of passenger services in 1954 and freight traffic a couple of years later.

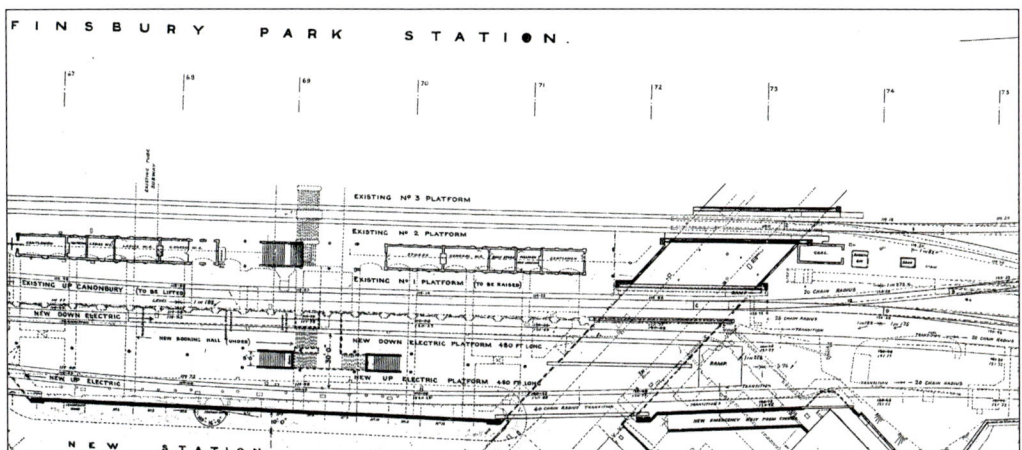

This plan shows the new high-level Northern line platforms adjacent to the existing Finsbury Park station. Drayton Park is to the left, while the route towards Highgate is on the right. Much of the steelwork for the new platforms was constructed, although the bridges over Seven Sisters Road and Stroud Green Road were not installed. The structure was later demolished. (Copyright TfL from the TfL Engineering Records Collection)

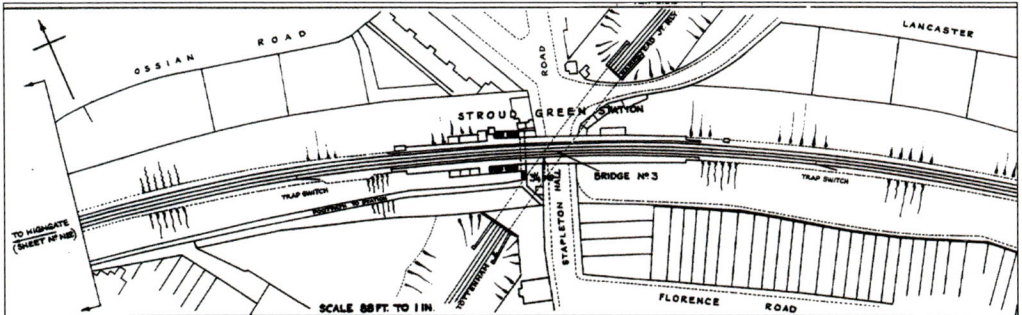

A plan showing Stroud Green station, prepared by London Transport for the Northern line electrification project. At this point the railway crossed the Tottenham and Hampstead Railway, now part of the London Overground, which has a station at Crouch Hill. (Copyright TfL from the TfL Engineering Records Collection)

The abandoned platforms at Crouch End, now part of a Parkland Walk, November 2013 (Malcolm Batten).

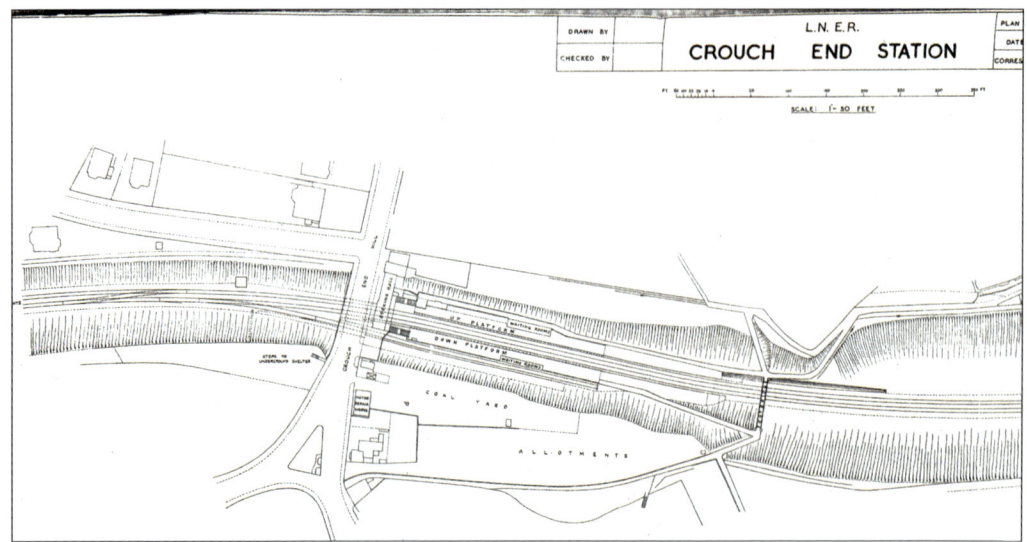

Crouch End station, dated 4 February 1946. The substation was located between Crouch End and Stroud Green to the right of the drawing, alongside Crouch Hill, and still survives today. (Copyright TfL from the TfL Engineering Records Collection)

The substation at Crouch End seen in November 1986.

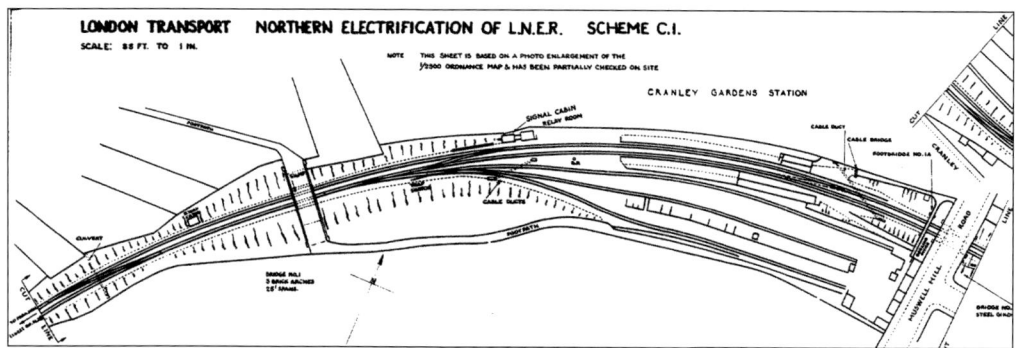

This drawing shows Cranley Gardens station. Conductor rails and cable runs were installed along most of the route between Finsbury Park and Alexandra Palace before the electrification scheme was abandoned. Most of the stations on the former LNER lines had goods yards that would have remained open when Northern line services commenced. (Copyright TfL from the TfL Engineering Records Collection)

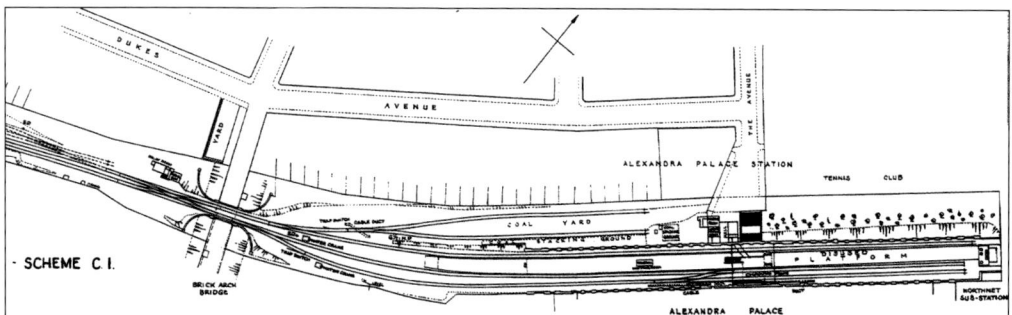

A plan showing Alexandra Palace station, prepared by London Transport for the Northern line electrification project. The station building at Alexandra Palace survives and is in use as a community centre. (Copyright TfL from the TfL Engineering Records Collection)

Mill Hill East, Edgware and the Elstree extension

As with the Alexandra Palace branch, work was started on upgrading the line, which would have seen the original Edgware LNER station abandoned and new connections installed to connect the route with Edgware underground station. Passenger services between Finchley Central and Edgware were withdrawn and replaced by a bus service in September 1939 to facilitate the construction works. Double track was installed between Finchley Central and Mill Hill The Hale, and the second platform at Mill Hill The Hale was partly constructed. Cabling was installed along much of the route together with some conductor rails. New substations were built at Page Street (between Mill Hill East and Mill Hill The Hale) and Edgware. Only one line was electrified between Finchley Central and Mill Hill East, with the newly installed second track between Finchley Central and Mill Hill The Hale being largely lifted between 1942 and 1943.

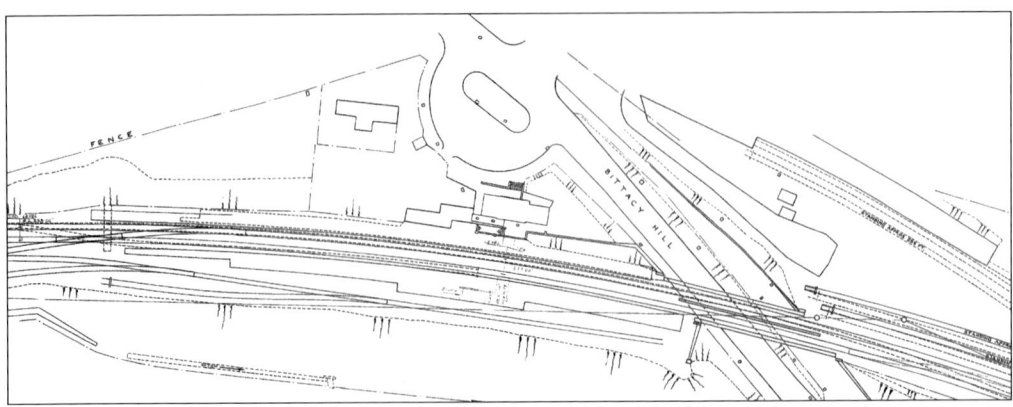

Mill Hill East station would have been rebuilt with two platforms. The original single wooden platform would have been replaced and extended as part of the works. At that time, there were goods yards in use at both end of the station, including sidings serving Mill Hill barracks. (Copyright TfL from the TfL Engineering Records Collection)

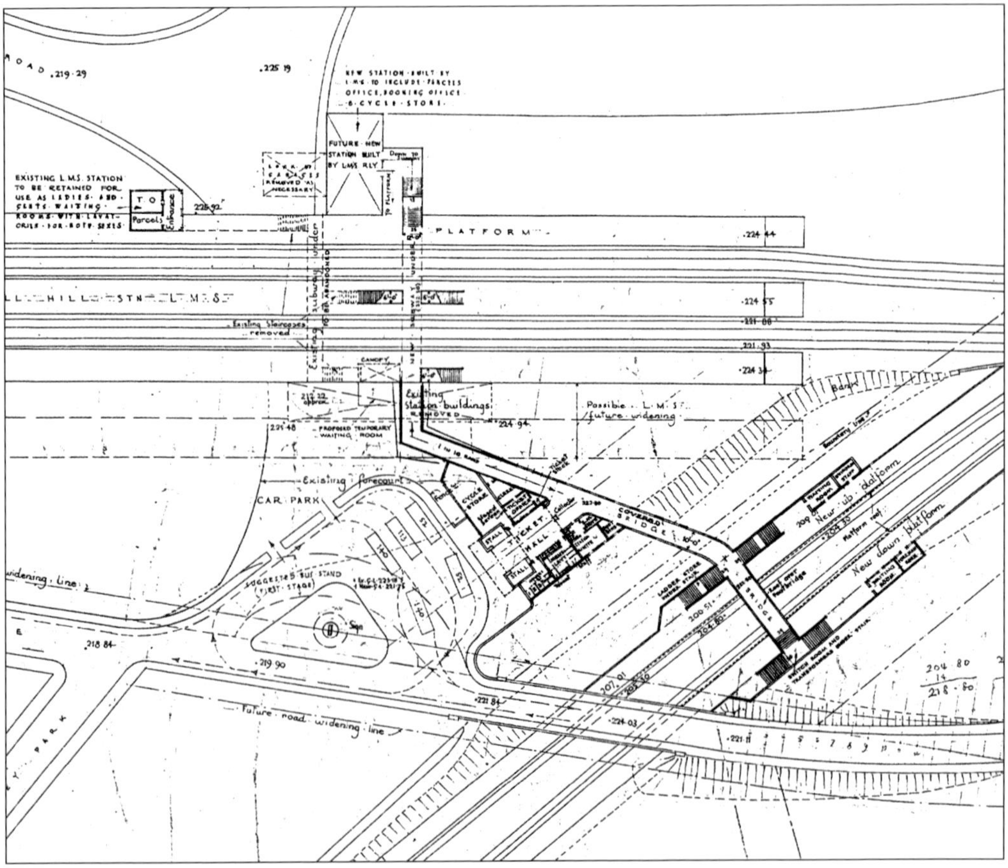

Mill Hill The Hale was originally built with a single platform, which was due for reconstruction. A majority of the second platform was constructed as part of the New Works Programme, although the interchange with the Mill Hill LMS station (now called Mill Hill Broadway) and the new station buildings were not completed. Mill Hill LMS station had four platforms, although the plan notes that there was land reserved for future widening. (Copyright TfL from the TfL Engineering Records Collection)

Edgware station

Edgware station was built with provision for a northern extension towards Elstree. A row of shops on Station Road and a service road (later renamed Rectory Lane) were constructed on a raft in order to facilitate the future extension.

Edgware was built with two platforms when it first opened in 1924. A third platform was added in 1932. The first plans for Edgware associated with the New Works Programme were drawn up in 1936, and included two platforms for Northern City and Highgate trains via Mill Hill East, and three platforms for the Edgware to Morden line trains via Golders Green. Five stabling sidings would have been provided alongside the Edgware and Morden line platforms in addition to the existing depot and sidings. A further six sidings would have been created in the space between the Golders Green and Mill Hill routes along with another six sidings adjacent to the Golders Green route.

Following authorisation of the Elstree extension in 1937, plans for Edgware were reconsidered to provide easier interchange between the Mill Hill East and Golders Green routes. This included the provision of a second route between Edgware and the Golders Green branch, and a new flyover enabling trains from the Mill Hill direction to cross over the second route from Golders Green, and provide a cross-platform interchange. Another platform was provided for trains terminating at Edgware from the Golders Green direction. The plans included four stabling sidings between the northbound line from Mill Hill East and the original route towards Golders Green.

Significant work was completed at Edgware, including the flyover for northbound trains from the Mill Hill East route, and the second route towards Golders Green, although this was not connected at the Golders Green end and was later used as stabling sidings until 1964.

A view of Edgware looking towards London, taken in September 1926. The original underground station and four-road depot can be seen to the left, as well as the route towards Watford (bottom left) and the raft that was built above the trackbed when the shops and service road (later renamed Rectory Lane) were constructed. The original GNR (*LNER) route to Edgware can be seen crossing the top right-hand corner of the photograph. (Copyright TfL from the London Transport Museum Collection).

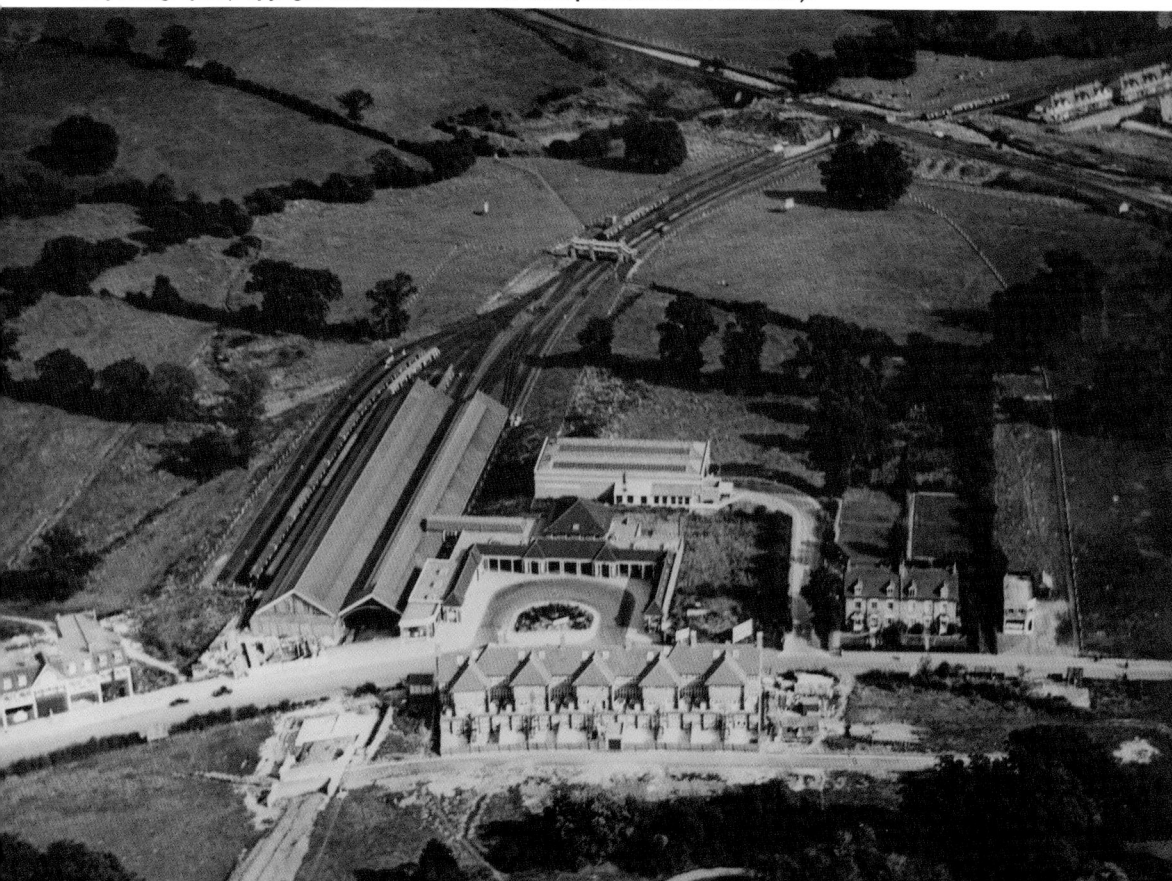

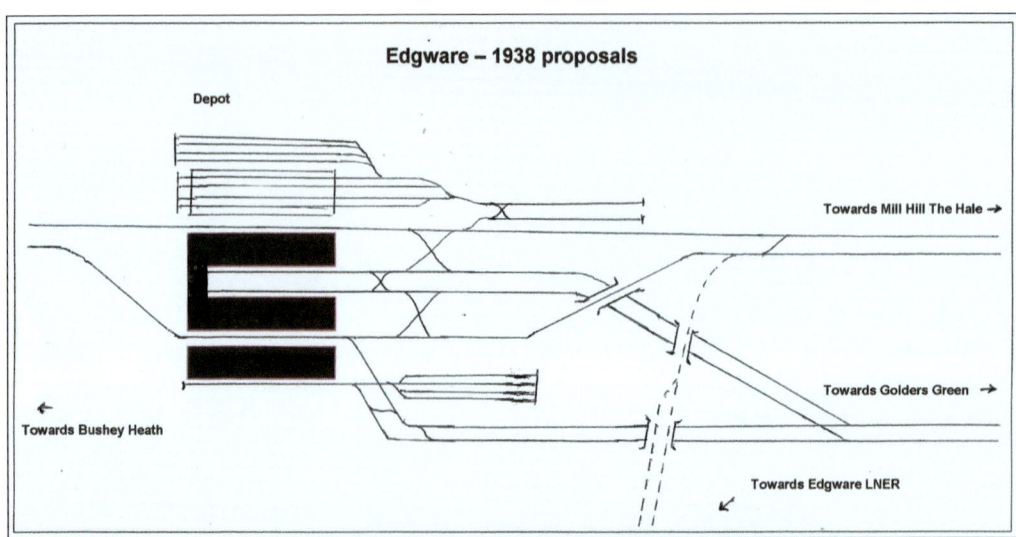

This is the final plan for Edgware station, dated 1938. Some of the work was completed before the entire project was abandoned in 1954. Trains today use the lower route between Golders Green and Edgware. The second route was never completed, although the trackbed was used for a couple of sidings until September 1964.

The original plan for Edgware, drawn up in 1936 before the Elstree extension had been authorised, provided two platforms for services via Mill Hill East and three for services via Golders Green. The Northern City and Highgate platforms, for the route via Mill Hill, included provision for a future extension towards Bushey Heath or Watford. Five sidings were proposed alongside the Edgware and Morden line platforms. (Copyright TfL from the TfL Engineering Records Collection)

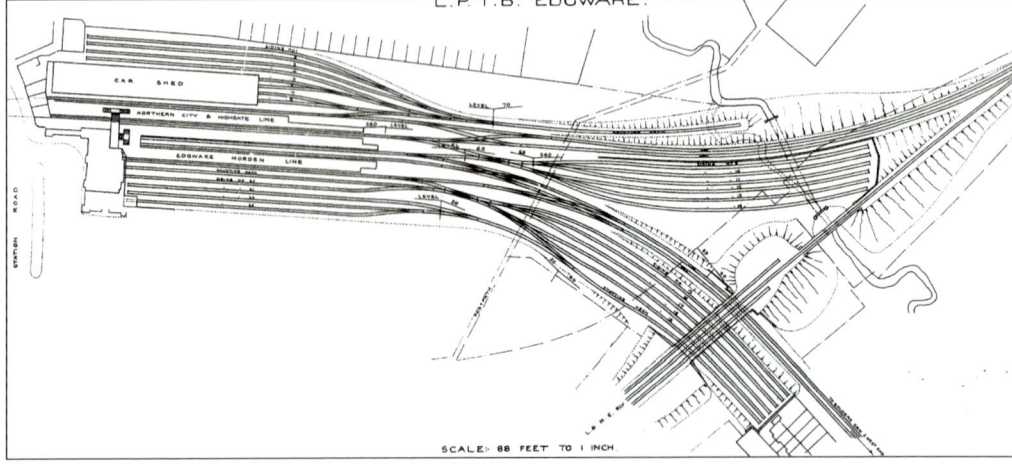

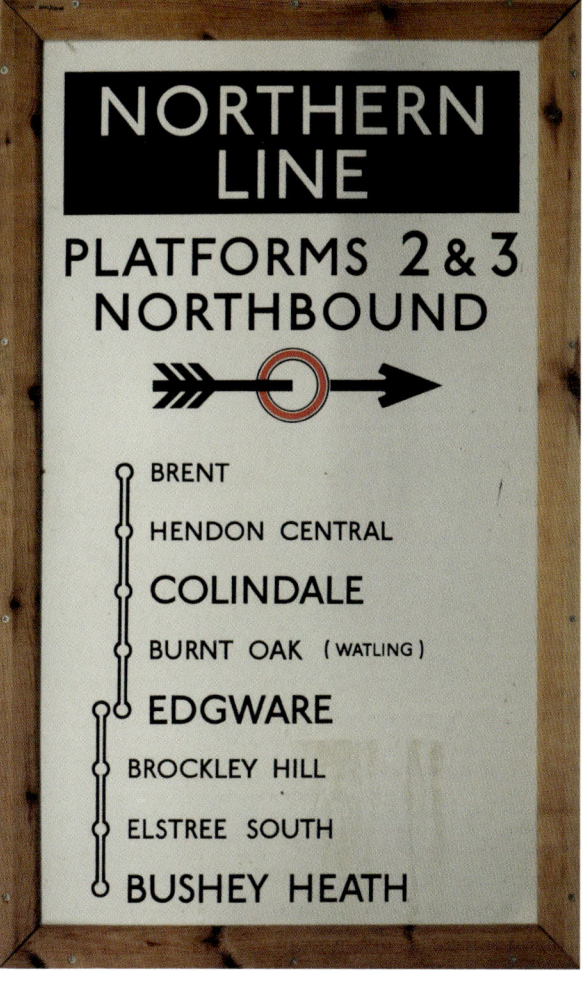

Right: Signage was installed at various locations along the Northern line in readiness for the new extensions. This map was installed at Edgware, indicating that passengers from the Golders Green route would normally need to change at Edgware to reach Bushey Heath, as trains on the Bushey Heath route would usually operate via Mill Hill East. (Copyright TfL from the London Transport Museum Collection)

Below left: A number of options were drawn up for Edgware station. This plan envisaged a completely new station building, incorporating a bus depot and a tower, but was not progressed. (Copyright TfL from the TfL Engineering Records Collection)

Below right: Another plan proposed a new circular ticket hall, along with a tower, to replace the original station building. This was not progressed. (Copyright TfL from the TfL Engineering Records Collection)

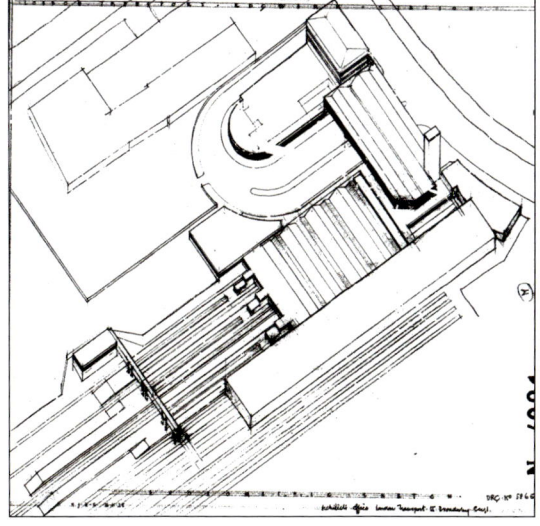

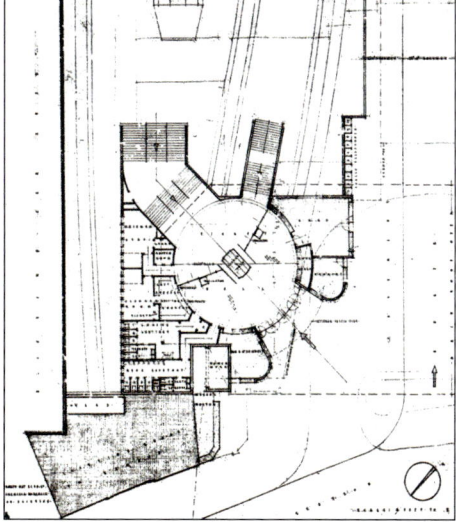

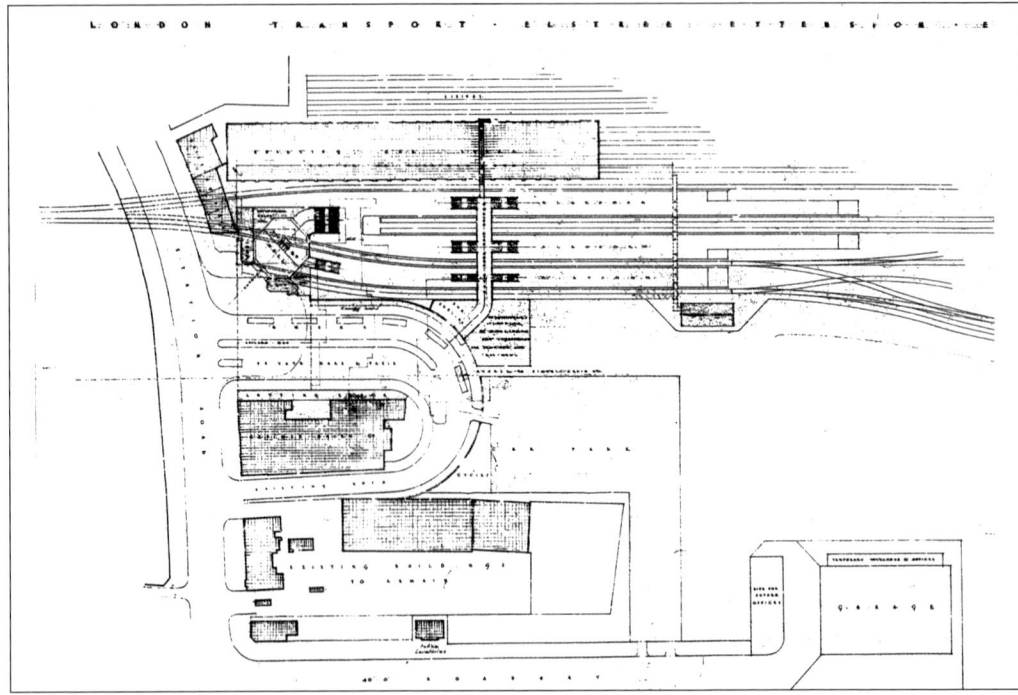

Another plan for Edgware station, showing the two bay platforms that would have been used by trains to and from the Golders Green branch. These were located between the southbound and northbound platforms, serving trains between Bushey Heath and London via the Mill Hill East route. A further bay platform, at the bottom of the plan, would also have been used by trains to and from the Golders Green branch, providing five tracks and six platforms in total. The platform layout was retained as shown, but the station buildings were subject to a further proposal, shown below. (Copyright TfL from the TfL Engineering Records Collection)

The final plans for Edgware station, dated 27 February 1940, retain much of the original station building. (Copyright TfL from the TfL Engineering Records Collection)

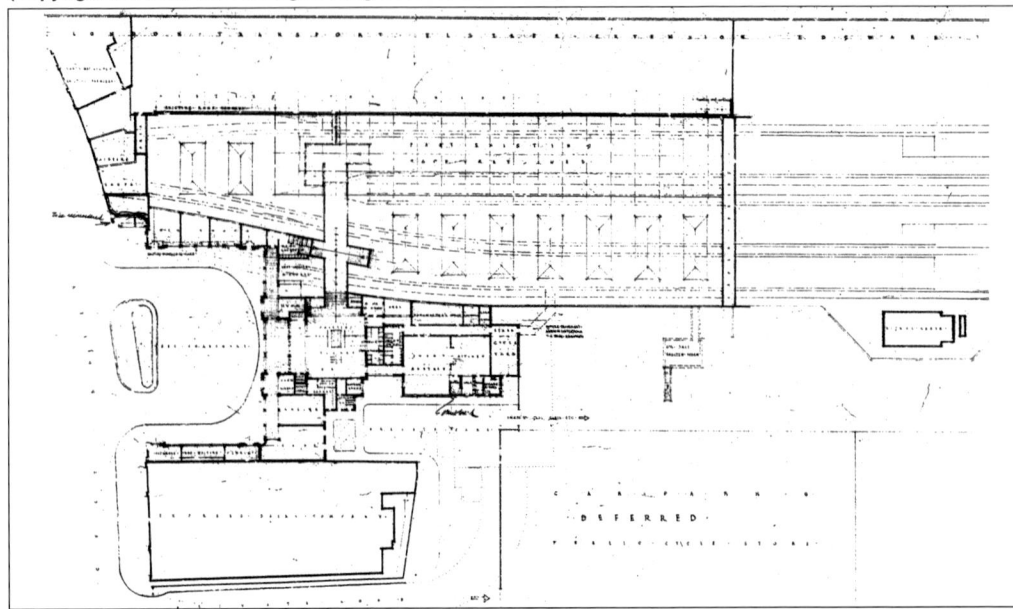

Edgware to Bushey Heath

The route beyond Edgware had been protected several years beforehand and some enabling works had taken place. Most of the route between Edgware and Brockley Hill was fenced and prepared for construction before work was stopped. At Brockley Hill work started on both sides of the Watford Bypass, including the viaduct that would have supported the new station and service road. Work also commenced on the Elstree Hill tunnels, near the site of Elstree South station, where foundations were also built for a new substation.

Beyond Elstree South no significant work was undertaken other than the construction of Aldenham Depot.

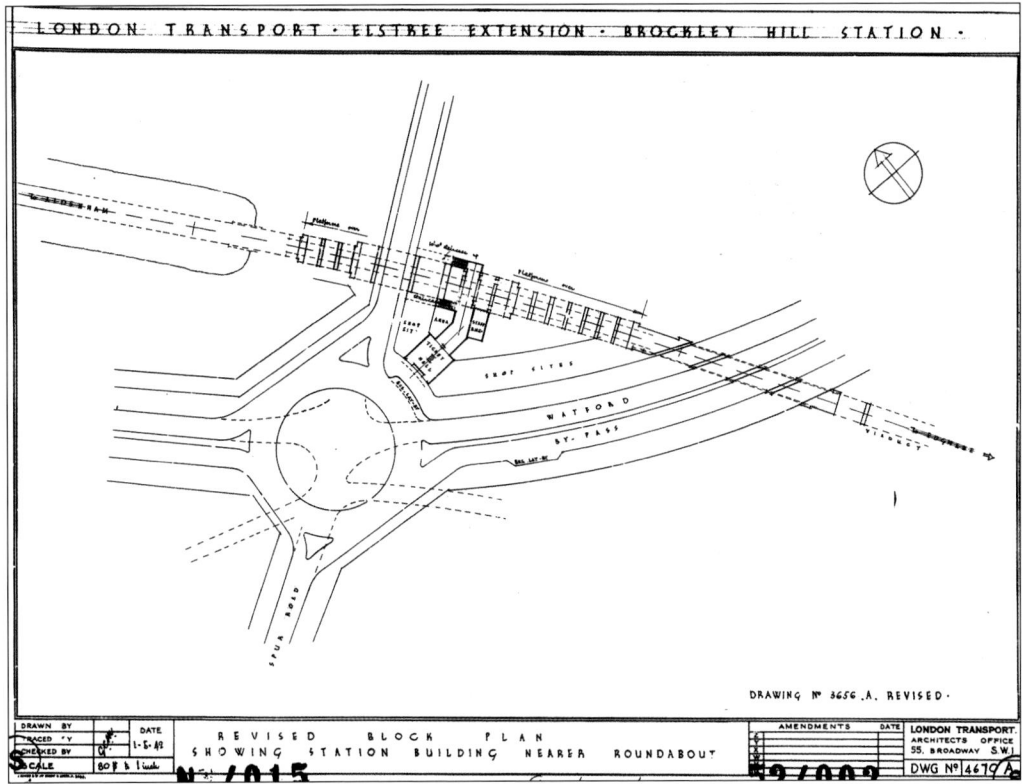

A plan of the proposed Brockley Hill station dated 2 November 1942. The viaduct was partly constructed on both sides of the Watford Bypass (now called Edgware Way). Some remains of the viaduct can still be seen today in the undergrowth. (Copyright TfL from the TfL Engineering Records Collection)

The Elstree and Borehamwood Museum held an exhibition during 2022 detailing the proposed Northern line extension to Bushey Heath, including a working model railway with stations resembling the proposed new stations. This is a model of Brockley Hill station taken on 29 January 2022.

A model of Elstree South station displayed at the Elstree and Borehamwood Museum on 29 January 2022. The model is now displayed at the Epping Signal Box Museum.

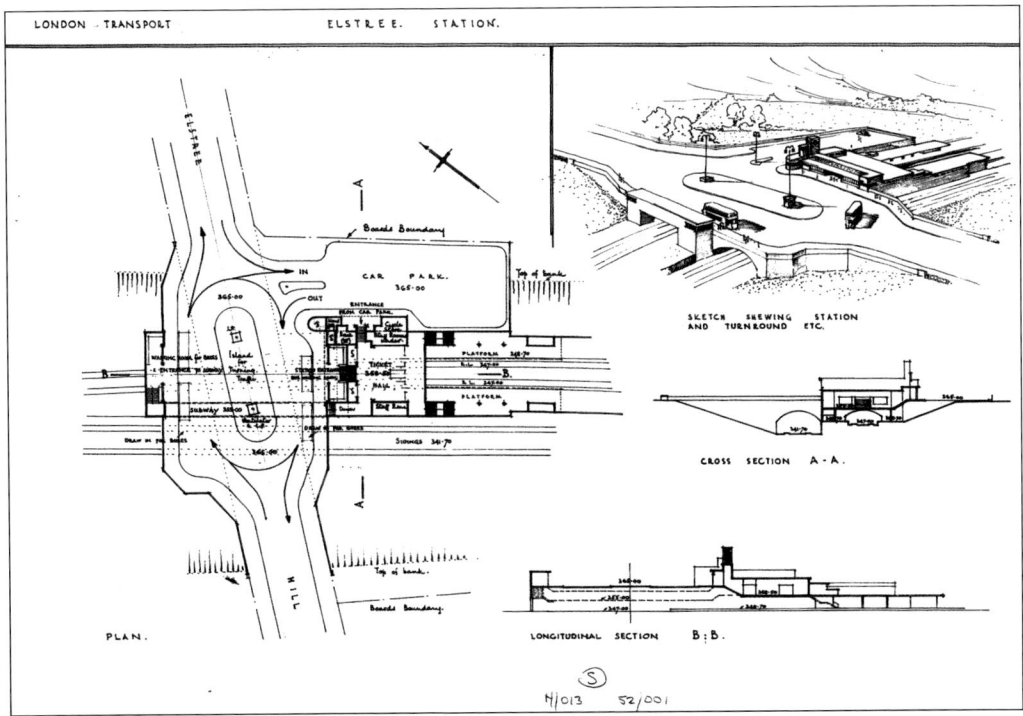

This drawing of Elstree South station, dated 2 December 1944, includes a scheme for widening the road to permit reversal of buses, as well as a subway connection from the ticket hall to a bus stand on the opposite side of Elstree Hill. There are two platforms, which are on a slightly higher level than the adjacent pair of tracks, which are depot reversing sidings. (Copyright TfL from the TfL Engineering Records Collection)

The station at Bushey Heath was originally called Aldenham, and would have consisted of three tracks, with four platform faces (similar in design to Cockfosters and Uxbridge stations). The name was changed to Bushey Heath in March 1938. The proposed station site was subsequently moved to a different alignment, with four tracks instead of three, and designed as a through station to enable a future extension towards Watford.

Signalling and power supply

Existing signal boxes were modified for London Transport use, with new facilities constructed or proposed at a number of locations including Drayton Park, Park Junction, East Finchley, Finchley Central, High Barnet, Edgware, Elstree Hill and Bushey Heath. Ground frames were also retained at a number of stations where good yards were in operation.

New sub-stations were planned at Elstree (partly built, but later demolished), Edgware, Mill Hill Page Street (built, but later demolished), High Barnet, Woodside Park, Finchley Central, East Finchley, Muswell Hill (built, but later demolished), Crouch End (still in place) and Drayton Park.

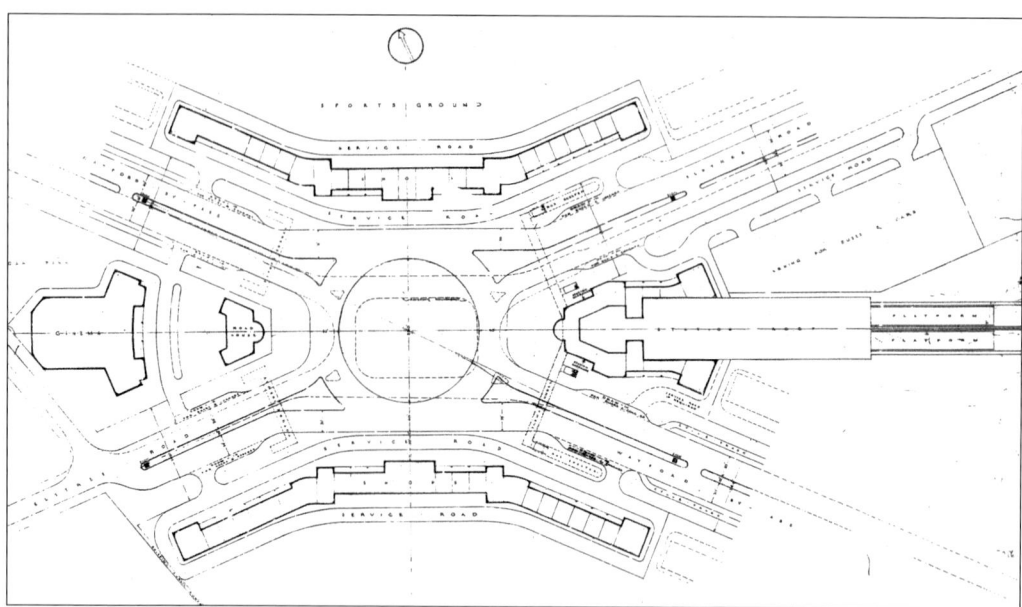

This plan, dated 1937, shows the original Aldenham station site. The station would have had three tracks and four platforms and would have been similar to Cockfosters and Uxbridge stations on the Piccadilly line. The proposed development around the station site includes shops, a road house and cinema. (Copyright TfL from the TfL Engineering Records Collection)

This plan shows two alternative sites for the station at Bushey Heath. In both cases the station is shown with three tracks and four platforms (and would have looked similar to Uxbridge and Cockfosters). The site to the top left-hand side of the plan was adopted, but redesigned with four tracks and four platforms. (Copyright TfL from the TfL Engineering Records Collection)

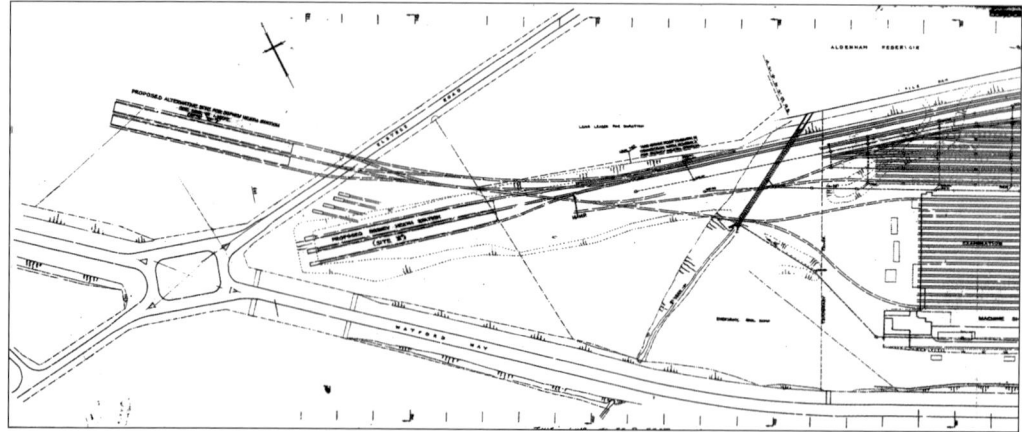

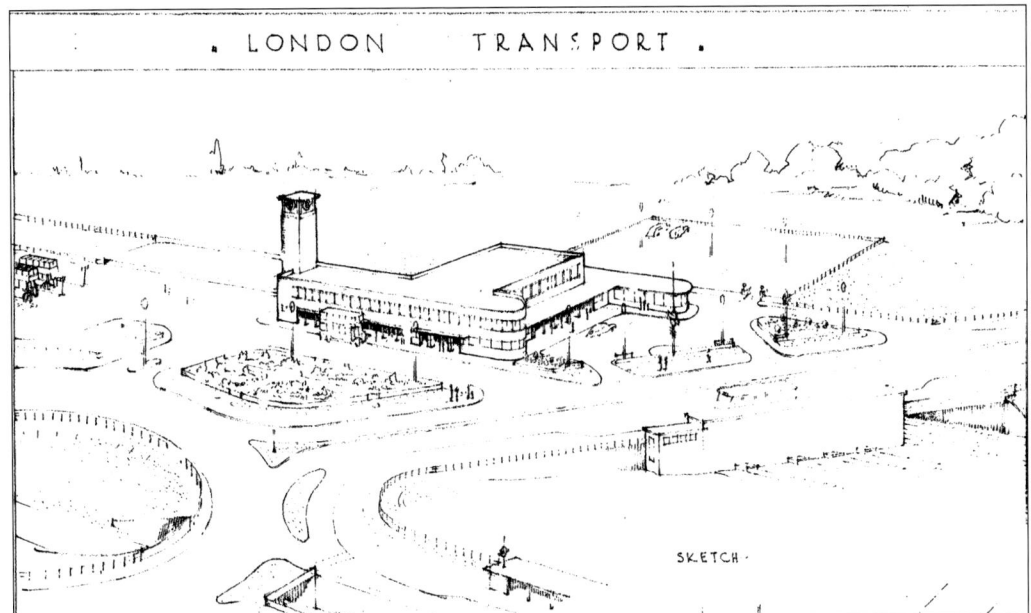

. LONDON   TRANSPORT .

SKETCH·

This post-war drawing shows the revised Bushey Heath station site. The station, which would have been provided with four platform tracks, was designed to enable a future extension towards Watford. (Copyright TfL from the TfL Engineering Records Collection)

Depot and sidings arrangements

The small depot at Drayton Park was retained as part of the 1935–1940 New Works Programme, and remained in operation until 1966, when it became a stabling location only.

The Wellington Sidings at Highgate were remodelled and renamed Highgate Depot. New sidings were provided alongside the Alexandra Palace branch called Highgate Wood Sidings (although not all works were completed). Stabling sidings were also provided at Edgware and High Barnet in addition to the new depot at Aldenham. Under the final proposals the depot at Golders Green would have been used for stabling, with most of the maintenance activities moving to the new facility at Aldenham.

Several alternative depots sites were considered including a site at Page Street between Mill Hill East and Mill Hill The Hale and a site at Finchley Manor between East Finchley and Finchley Central. Another location considered was just north of Burnt Oak.

Post-World War Two developments

Immediately after World War Two, it was assumed that the extensions would all be completed, with Mill Hill East to Edgware expected to be open by June 1948, and all works at Edgware station completed by August 1949. However, in part due to newly introduced Green Belt legislation, plans for the Bushey Heath extension were abandoned in November 1950. It was announced that the extension from Mill Hill East to either Mill Hill The Hale or Edgware might progress at a later date, and there was the possibility of a short extension from Edgware to Brockley Hill. A further update was issued in February 1954, confirming that all the uncompleted works would be abandoned.

Brockley Hill viaduct was partly demolished in 1959 and the partly built tunnels at Elstree were buried under the M1. The trackbed near Mill Hill The Hale was also severed by the M1. Aldenham Depot, used for aircraft production during World War Two, was converted into a bus and coach overhaul works between 1952 and 1956. The works were in use until 1986, when the facility was no longer required.

The passenger service between Finsbury Park and Alexandra Palace, passing through the rebuilt Highgate (high-level) station, continued until 5 July 1954. Freight services lasted a little longer, operating to Muswell Hill until 14 June 1956, and Cranley Gardens until 18 May 1957. High Barnet goods yard closed on 1 October 1962. Freight traffic between Finsbury Park, Park Junction and Edgware (GNR/LNER station) lasted until 1 June 1964. Most of the conductor rails were removed in the mid-1950s with some utilised elsewhere on the network.

Until September 1970, the route between Finsbury Park and Park Junction remained open for rolling stock transfers to and from the Northern City line. These were hauled by London Transport battery locomotives, but from 1970, services were rerouted from Finsbury Park via King's Cross (suburban) and the Widened Lines to Farringdon where they crossed to the Metropolitan line and then onwards to their final destination. The line between Finsbury Park and Park Junction was lifted by 1972.

Edgware station was partly rebuilt for the proposed extensions. In 1954, there was a scheme to use the eastern pair of tracks to reach Edgware station, rather than the original route from Golders Green, along with the construction of some additional sidings but the scheme was not progressed.

In 1966, platforms 2 and 3 were extended beneath Station Road at Edgware, with some further changes made in 1977 following the Moorgate accident in February 1975. The flyover that was to take northbound Mill Hill East branch trains over the second Golders Green route was eventually demolished in 1996 to make way for additional sidings at Edgware to accommodate new 1995 rolling stock.

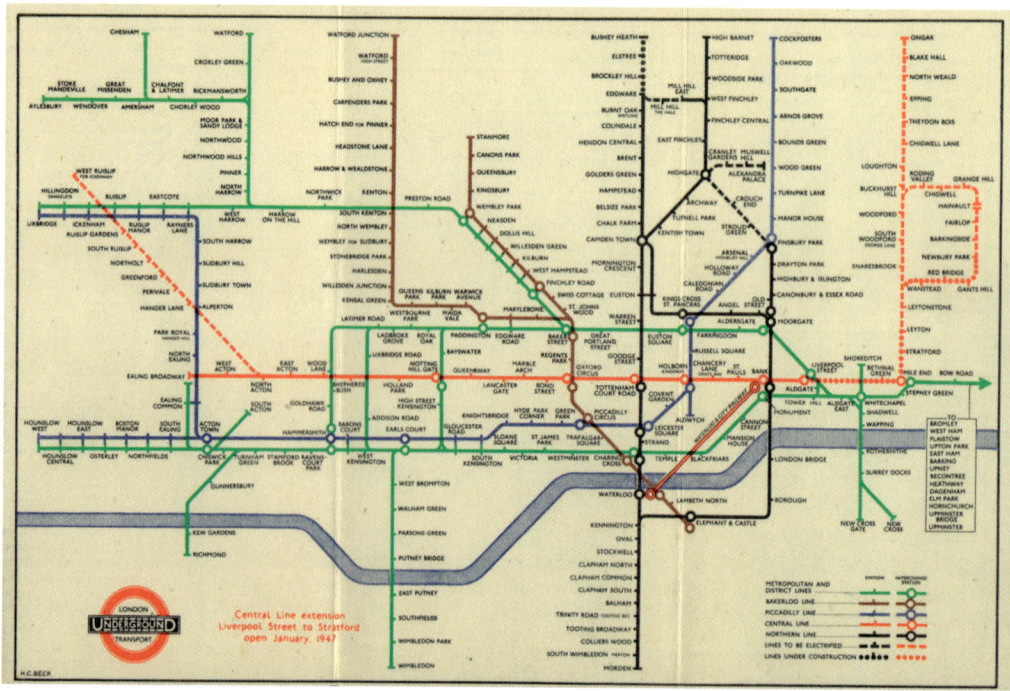

The 1946 Underground Map included the proposed extensions between Finsbury Park and Alexandra Palace via Highgate, and between Mill Hill East and Bushey Heath, both of which were subsequently abandoned. (Copyright TfL from the London Transport Museum Collection)

The route today

Most of the route between Alexandra Palace and Finsbury Park is now a parkland walk. The former station building at Alexandra Palace is a community centre, while the high-level platforms at Highgate can still be seen between the trees, although the tunnels at each end have been sealed. The former platforms at Crouch End can still be seen as well as the nearby substation and the former Stationmaster's House at Stroud Green.

Parts of the route between Edgware and Mill Hill East can still be traced, some of which is now the Mill Hill Old Railway Nature Reserve.

Some evidence of the additional island platform at Edgware can also be seen as well as the route of the proposed railway just north of Edgware station. On the Bushey Heath extension, a few remaining stubs of brickwork are still visible at Brockley Hill.

The remains of the partly constructed viaduct at Brockley Hill station, seen on 29 January 2022.

In preparation for a future extension from Edgware towards Watford, a service road (later renamed Rectory Lane) was constructed on a raft. The parapet wall in June 1986.

Platforms 2 and 3 at Edgware looking towards Bushey Heath on June 1986, with trains of 1972 Stock in both platforms.

A view of Edgware station taken in November 1986, including the four-road depot building, the roof covering Platforms 2 and 3 and the more exposed Platform 1. On the left can be seen the end of the new island platform constructed as part of the 1935–1940 New Works Programme. The left-hand face would have been a bay platform for use by trains terminating at Edgware from the Golders Green direction, while the right-hand face would have been used by Bushey Heath services.

The end of the line at Mill Hill East, looking towards the abandoned route to Mill Hill The Hale and Edgware, on 23 July 2022.

Mill Hill East looking towards Finchley Central on 23 July 2022. The space for the second track, installed and electrified as part of the 1935–1940 New Works Programme, but subsequently removed, can be seen on Bittacy Hill bridge.

A train of 1995 Stock arrives in Platform 2 at East Finchley from Highgate Depot on 23 January 2016.

The tunnel mouths at Park Junction, looking towards Highgate, in November 1986. The right-hand portal was damaged in World War Two and subsequently repaired.

The tunnel portals at Highgate (high level) looking towards Finsbury Park in June 1986.

The abandoned Highgate (high level) platforms seen in June 1986. These platforms were used by passenger services between Finsbury Park and Alexandra Palace until 1954, freight services until 1964, and Northern line rolling stock transfers until 1970.

The staircase linking Highgate (high-level) platforms with the sub-surface concourse and low-level platforms, June 1986.

Highgate (low level) platforms were rebuilt as part of the 1935–1940 New Works Programme, including provision for nine-carriage trains, 23 January 2016.

Most of the route between Alexandra Palace and Highgate is now a parkland walk. The railway passes over a footpath at Alexandra Palace on 19 January 2020.

The station building at Alexandra Palace is now used as a community centre, with the majestic Alexandra Palace standing behind, 19 January 2020.

The remains of Crouch End station, including the staircase that provided access from Crouch End Hill, autumn 1986.

The disused platforms at Crouch End station. The platform heights were modified for use by underground rolling stock as part of the 1935–1940 New Works Programme, autumn 1986.

World War Two

A majority of stations across the deep-level underground network were used as shelters during World War Two. Initially the arrangements were unofficial, but they became more organised as the Blitz intensified during 1940. A number of stations on the Northern line were damaged during the air raids including Balham, Borough, Camden Town, Goodge Street and Tottenham Court Road. The tunnel mouth at the north end of Highgate (high-level) station was also damaged but was subsequently rebuilt.

The closed stations at South Kentish Town and City Road were reopened to provide shelter. The former King William Street station and a section of the abandoned tunnels were also used as an air raid shelter for Londoners. The partly constructed underground platforms at Highgate were also opened up.

Flood gates were installed at Waterloo, Charing Cross and London Bridge where the tunnels passed below the River Thames, to protect the underground system from flooding. The abandoned Embankment loop was also plugged to prevent the risk of flooding.

Express tubes and deep-level shelters

Plans for an express service were first proposed in 1935, with additional tunnels planned between Waterloo and Kentish Town, connecting with the Highgate branch just north of Camden Town, along with a possible connection to the Edgware branch. Intermediate stops were proposed at Charing Cross, Leicester Square and Tottenham Court Road. A branch to Finsbury Park was also suggested, connecting with the LNER network. The plans were later modified to provide express tunnels between Archway and Tottenham Court Road but without any intermediate stations.

In 1936, there were proposals to ease congestion on the Edgware branch by constructing a new link to Swiss Cottage and then via the new Bakerloo line tunnels (planned as part of the 1935–1940 New Works Programme) to Victoria via Baker Street. There were later plans for a new route from Golders Green or Finchley to Motspur Park or Chessington via Waterloo and Clapham to ease congestion on the Northern line.

In the early days of World War Two, plans were drawn up for a series of deep-level air raid shelters. They were located parallel to existing underground railways so that they could be converted into express tube lines after the war. Deep-level shelters were planned below the existing Northern line tunnels, at the following locations:

- Belsize Park
- Camden Town
- Goodge Street
- Oval (started but not finished due to poor ground conditions)
- Stockwell
- Clapham North
- Clapham Common
- Clapham South

Shelters were also planned alongside the Central line at Chancery Lane and St Pauls, although only Chancery Lane was completed.

The shelters were to consist of twin 1,400ft long, 16ft 6in diameter tunnels. Work started in 1941 and the shelters were completed in 1942. The shelters were used regularly from 1944, when German V1 flying bombs started to attack London. Some were later used as hostels and for migrant workers arriving in the country, including from the *Empire Windrush*. Seven of the eight shelters were sold to Transport for London in the 1990s and have subsequently been used for a variety of purposes.

Three express tube routes were considered:

- Bank to Holborn (parallel to the Central line).
- Camden Town to Tottenham Court Road.
- Kennington to Balham via Clapham Common.

Had the express tube schemes been progressed, it is likely that interchange stations would have been built at Kennington and Balham, with trains running non-stop between these locations.

The deep-level shelter entrance on Haverstock Hill at Belsize Park on 3 December 2022. The buildings are now used as a datastore.

The second entrance to the Belsize Park deep-level shelter, 3 December 2022.

Camden Town deep-level shelter, 29 January 2022.

The Goodge Street deep-level shelter entrance on Tottenham Court Road, 23 July 2022.

The Goodge Street deep-level shelter entrance on Chenies Street (known as the Eisenhower Centre) on 23 July 2022.

Stockwell deep-level shelter on 6 August 2016, having been painted in a colourful mural.

Clapham North deep-level shelter on 3 December 2022.

Clapham Common deep-level shelter on 6 August 2016.

Clapham Common deep-level shelter on 6 August 2016.

The entrance to Clapham South deep-level shelter in 1942. (Copyright TfL from the London Transport Museum Collection).

Clapham South deep-level shelter on 6 August 2016.

The London Plan

The County of London Plan was published in 1943 and set out the strategy for reconstruction of the city following World War Two, including housing, industry and public transport. A number of significant rail schemes were suggested in the initial report. A Working Party was established to carry out a detailed investigation and included members of the London Transport Executive.

London Plan Working Party

The Working Party examined proposals for a number of new underground lines including:

Route 1:   A new tunnel from Lewisham via Tower Bridge Road, Fenchurch Street to Moorgate linking Southern Region services via Forest Hill with the Northern City line at Moorgate. Through services would have operated to Alexandra Palace and Enfield Town. This would have required some modification to the arrangements at Finsbury Park, which at this point had been partly completed as part of the 1935–1940 New Works Programme.

Routes 10, 11, 12A and 12B all provided relief to the crowded Northern line as follows:

Route 10:   A new deep-level tube line between Kennington and Tooting.

Route 11:   An extension from Morden to North Cheam.

Route 12A: A new deep-level tube line between Golders Green and Waterloo, potentially utilising the shelters at Belsize Park, Camden Town and Goodge Street.

Route 12B: A new tube line between Finchley, Golders Green, Baker Street, Knightsbridge, Sloane Square and Clapham Junction.

The Working Party provided two progress reports on 21 January 1946 to the Minister of War Transport, and on the 3 March 1948 to the Minister of Transport, including details of the above proposals.

London Plan Working Party Report

The final London Plan Working Party Report was published in 1949 and provided a refinement of the proposals considered by the Working Party. The new routes were given letters instead of numbers to avoid confusion with the progress reports. The final report also provided comprehensive maps showing the proposed new lines. A selection of the maps, along with a summary of the proposals, were also published in the August 1949 London Transport staff magazine.

The final report recommended that the 1935–40 New Works Programme should be completed as a first priority, with the exception of the planned electrification between Stratford and Fenchurch Street. The report also suggested a review of the proposed method of operation of the line between Epping and Ongar.

The report suggested a number of new tube schemes, including:

Route E: This was a lower priority scheme to duplicate the Northern line from Kennington to Tooting Broadway (non-stop) then to South Wimbledon with two branches to Chessington South via Raynes Park and Motspur Park, and a second branch to North Cheam. This may have utilised the deep-level shelters in south London.

Schemes J and K were alternative options for a southern extension of the Northern City line from Moorgate.

Route J: Was from Moorgate to Dagenham via New Cross, Deptford, Woolwich and Plumsted. **Route K**: Was from Moorgate to Crystal Palace via Bricklayers Arms and Peckham.

Proposals to duplicate the Northern line between Waterloo and Golders Green, and a new route to Clapham Junction (routes 12A and 12B) were dropped as other schemes provided alternative capacity.

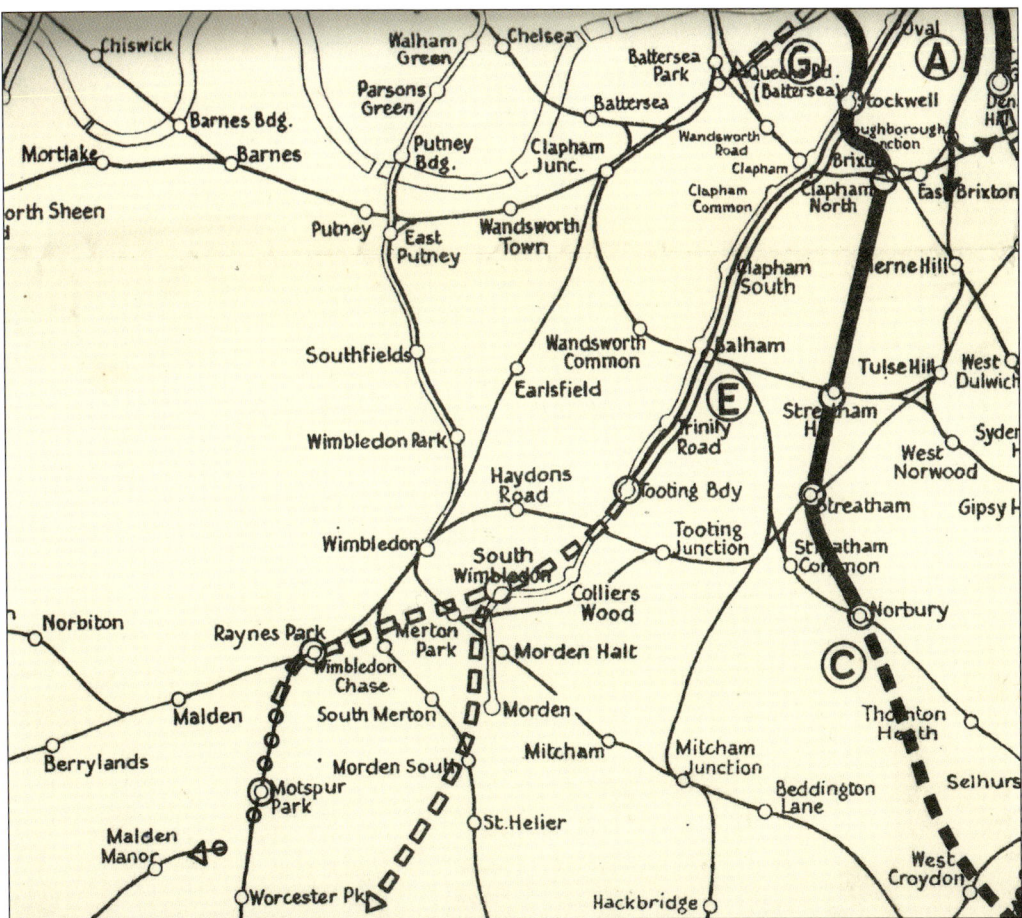

The final *London Plan Working Party Report* was published in 1949. This extract shows *Route E*, which was a lower priority scheme to duplicate the Northern line from Kennington to Tooting Broadway (non-stop) then to South Wimbledon with two branches to Chessington South and North Cheam (*London Plan Working Party Report*, 1949, used with permission)

Chapter 6

Abandoned Stations and Infrastructure

Brent (Cross)

Brent station opened on 19 November 1923 and was renamed Brent Cross on 20 July 1976 after the adjacent Brent Cross Shopping Centre. The station has an island platform and was built with provision for passing loops to be added. These came into use in January 1925 and were used by fast peak-hour trains, before being taken out of use on 23 August 1936. The location of the loops can still be seen today. Provision was also made for passing loops (in the London-bound direction) at Colindale and Burnt Oak, but the third track was not installed.

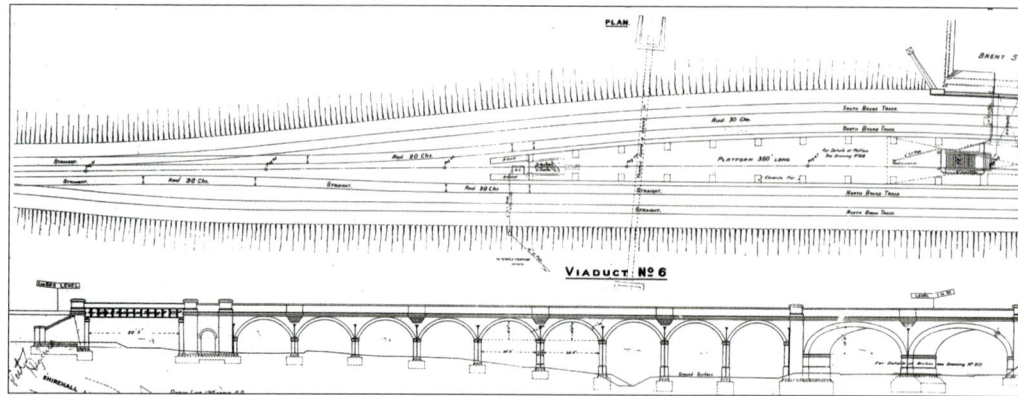

A Plan of Brent station (now Brent Cross) showing the Hendon end of the station, including the northbound and southbound passing loops. The loops were installed a few years after the station opened and were used by non-stop trains until being taken out of use in 1936. (Copyright TfL from the TfL Engineering Records Collection)

A view of two southbound trains passing at Brent on 18 June 1927. There were loops in both directions, the site of which can still be seen today. (Copyright TfL from the London Transport Museum Collection)

Brent Cross station on 25 July 2018, looking towards London. The location of the passing loops can clearly be seen on each side of the running lines.

A train of 1995 Stock arriving in the northbound platform at Brent Cross with an Edgware train on 29 January 2022. The location of the former loop can be seen to the right of the train.

City Road

City Road was located between Angel and Old Street. The station was opened by the City and South London Railway on 17 November 1901. Passenger numbers were low and the station closed on 8 August 1922, when the line was closed to enlarge the tunnels. The station was used as an air raid shelter during World War Two. Most of the station buildings were demolished in the 1960s, with a small section remaining where the old lift shaft was located (which provided ventilation to the tunnels below, long after the station closed). The remaining sections of the station building were removed and replaced with the Bunhill 2 Energy Centre, which uses heat from the Underground to warm local houses and a school.

A view of City Road station taken in 1915, seven years before closure. (Copyright TfL from the London Transport Museum Collection)

The remains of City Road station, by this time acting as a ventilation shaft for the Northern line tunnels below, on 14 June 1999. The station was opened by the City & South London Railway in 1901, but closed in 1922 when the original narrow tunnels were closed for enlargement.

The site of City Road station on 29 January 2022. The building is called the Bunhill 2 Energy Centre, which uses heat from the Underground to warm local buildings.

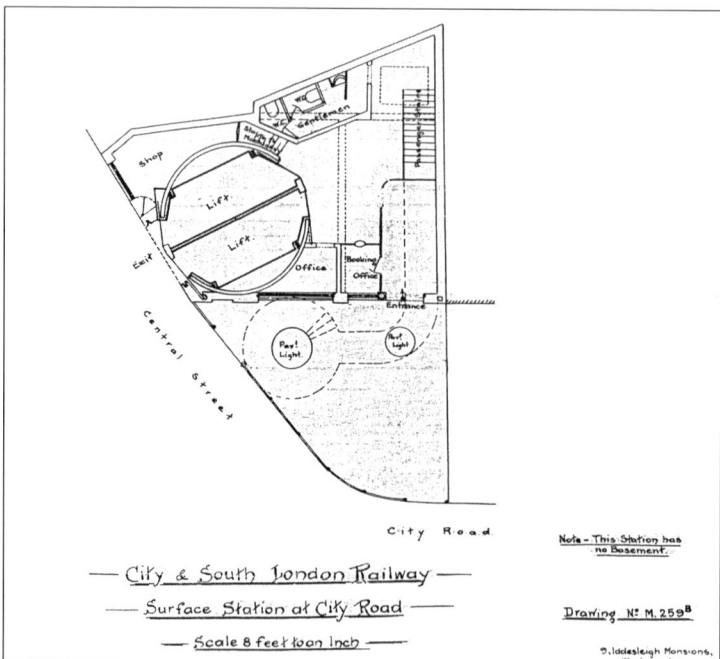

A plan showing the surface-level building at City Road, which was constructed by the City & South London Railway. The station had two lifts located in a single lift shaft. (Copyright TfL from the TfL Engineering Records Collection)

Embankment loop

The Charing Cross, Euston and Hampstead Railway opened as far as Charing Cross on 22 June 1907. A further extension to Charing Cross (Embankment), now Embankment, was opened on 6 April 1914. This provided a connection with the District Railway at Embankment. The extension consisted of a single-track loop that passed beneath the River Thames. The single platform is now the northbound platform at Embankment. The loop was subsequently abandoned when the line was extended to Kennington on 13 September 1926, when a southbound platform was added at Embankment. The remainder of the loop was plugged in 1939 as there were concerns about the tunnel being damaged and causing flooding to the underground network. The former loop line was later bombed, so this proved to be a sensible decision.

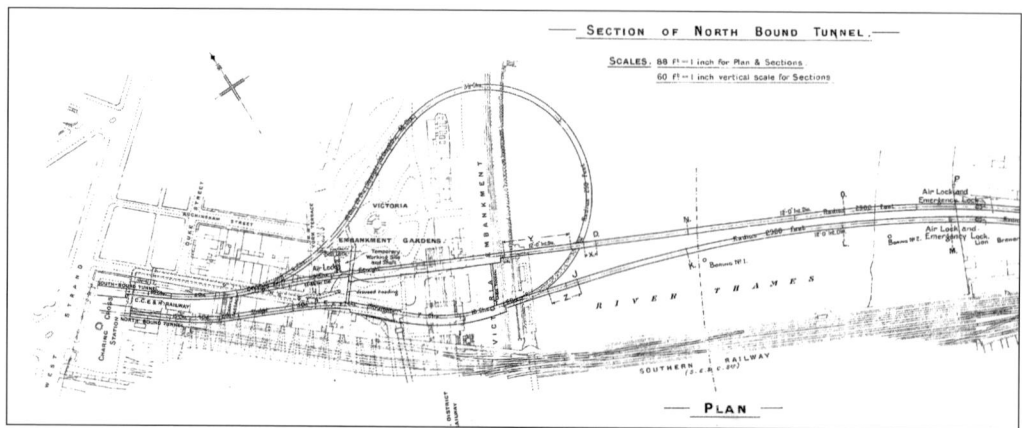

This 1924 drawing shows the extension from Embankment to Kennington, which resulted in the closure of the Embankment loop. The new southbound platform can be seen as well as the curved northbound platform, which was retained as part of the extension. (Copyright TfL from the TfL Engineering Records Collection)

Euston

The City and South London Railway opened its Euston station on 12 May 1907 with a building on Seymour Street (now Eversholt Street). It closed on 30 September 1914 and was demolished in 1934. The Charing Cross, Euston and Hampstead Railway opened its station at Euston on 22 June 1907 on Melton Street. This also closed on 30 September 1914, but was retained as a ventilation shaft and emergency exit. An interconnecting tunnel was constructed between the two stations, which included an underground ticket office. The original City & South London Railway platforms (on the Bank branch) were closed between 9 August 1922 and 20 April 2024 for rebuilding. The interconnection tunnel was closed on 29 April 1962 as part of the modernisation of the station and construction of the Victoria line. The Charing Cross, Euston and Hampstead Railway building is due to be demolished as part of the HS2 construction works at Euston.

The Charing Cross, Euston and Hampstead Railway station at Euston, designed by Leslie Green and opened on 17 June 2016. The building is due to be demolished to make way for the new HS2 station at Euston.

King William Street

King William Street had a very short life. It was opened on 18 December 1890 and closed on 24 February 1900, when the line was extended to Moorgate Street. During this short period the original side platforms were replaced with an island platform in 1895. The old station saw further use as an air raid shelter during World War Two.

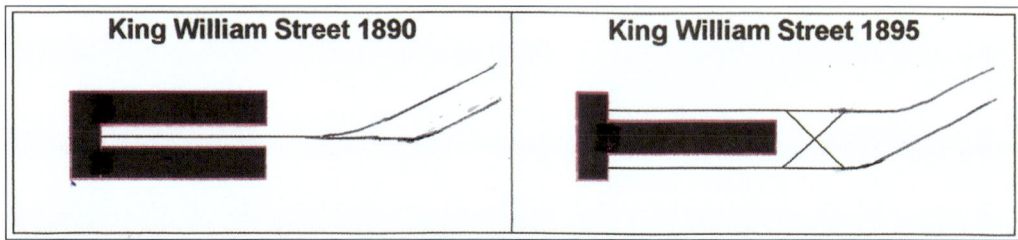

King William Street was initially constructed with a single track and two side platforms. To increase capacity the station was rebuilt in 1895 with two tracks and a narrow island platform, before closing five years later.

An original plan for King William Street showing the single platform line with separate arrival and departure platforms. (Copyright TfL from the TfL Engineering Records Collection)

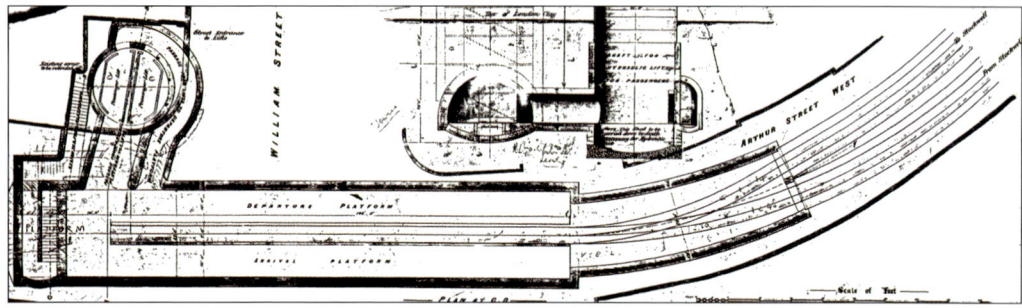

A view of the abandoned platforms at King William Street in 1930. (Copyright TfL from the London Transport Museum Collection)

North End (Bull & Bush)

North End station would have been located between Hampstead and Golders Green, deep beneath Hampstead Heath. Work started on the station in 1903 with the station tunnels and passageways constructed. Due to planning issues the proposed residential developments did not progress and there was also local opposition to the station. Work was eventually stopped in 1906 before the lift shafts and surface building had been completed.

During World War Two the underground passageways were used to store important documents.

In the mid-1950s, an underground control room was constructed to operate a series of floodgates located around the underground network. The control room was connected to the surface by a lift shaft and stairs and a surface-level entrance was provided. This secret facility was eventually closed and today the shaft and surface-level buildings are used as an emergency escape shaft. Although the proposed station was officially called North End, it is often referred to as Bull and Bush, due to a local pub of the same name.

In 1978, the platforms were used as a worksite for the removal of 430 yards of blue asbestos that had been installed in the southbound tunnel between Golders Green and Hampstead in 1932 as an experiment to improve soundproofing.

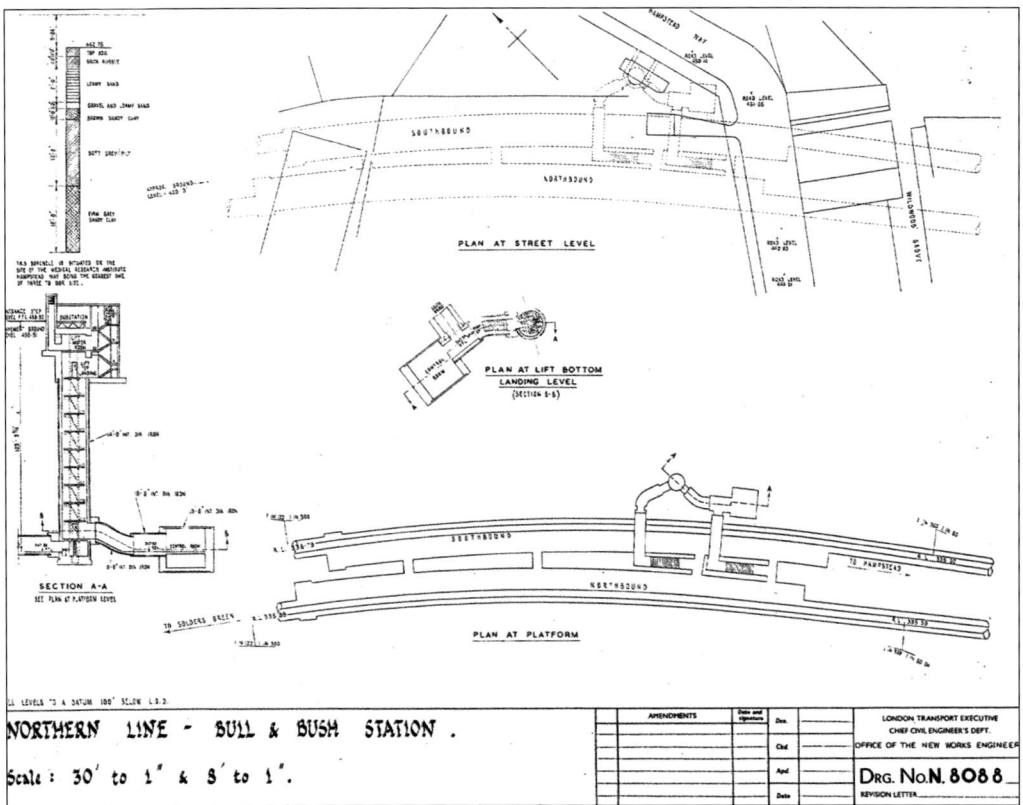

This drawing shows the shaft and control room that was constructed in the 1950s to link the underground station with the surface. The control room managed the operation of floodgates across the underground network. Although the station was officially called North End, the more informal name of Bull & Bush has been used on this drawing. (Copyright TfL from the TfL Engineering Records Collection)

The entrance to the emergency escape shaft at North End (Bull & Bush), which was planned as a station on the Northern line between Hampstead and Golders Green, on 29 January 2022.

South Kentish Town

South Kentish Town was initially referred to as Castle Road, the latter name being included on some platform tiling, but the station opened as South Kentish Town on 22 June 1907. The station was always fairly quiet and closed on 5 June 1924 following a strike at Lots Road Power Station. The station building can still be seen today and is currently used as retail space.

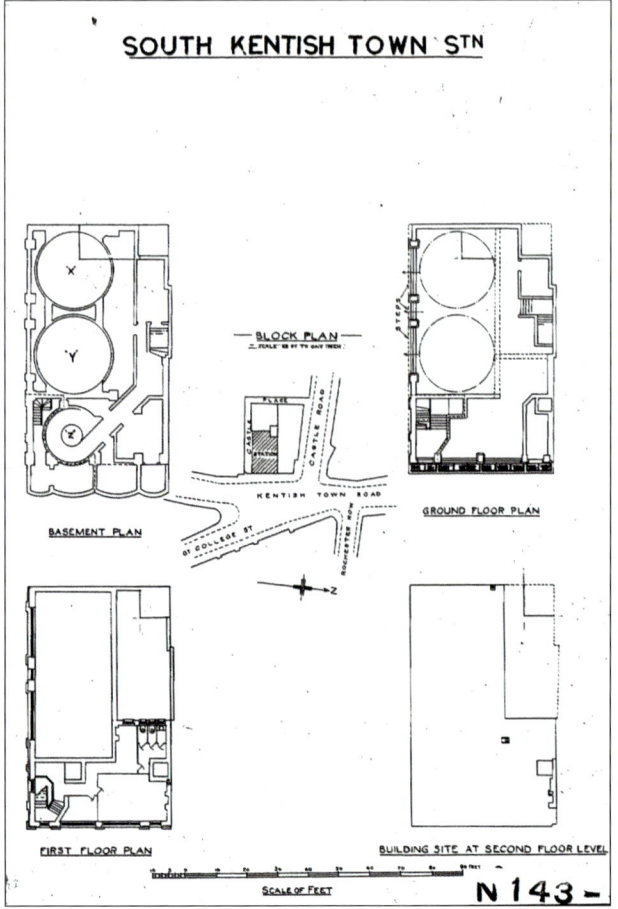

A plan of South Kentish Town station, which opened in 1907 but closed in 1924. It was originally going to be called Castle Road, after the street that runs parallel with the station. (Copyright TfL from the TfL Engineering Records Collection)

The former station at South Kentish Town is still recognisable almost 100 years after it closed. This photograph was taken on 7 February 2016.

Stockwell

Stockwell station was constructed by the City & South London Railway and opened on 18 December 1890. The station consisted of an island platform with two side tracks. There was a crossover at the end of the platforms and a siding leading to a steep ramp up to Stockwell Depot. A siding, looping around the station, was added in later years to provide additional stabling capacity. As part of the works to enlarge the original tunnels, Stockwell station was rebuilt slightly to the south of the original location. The station closed on 28 November 1923 and reopened on 1 December 1924 following reconstruction.

Further changes were made to the station in the 1960s and early 1970s in preparation for the Victoria line, including a new, rather austere, surface building, which opened in 1971.

Chapter 7
Rolling Stock

The City & South London Railway

The City & South London Railway opened in 1890 and was the first underground railway to use electric traction. In total, 14 locomotives were originally provided, which increased to 52 by 1901. The initial batch of locomotives were built by Mather & Platt Engineers. Locomotives 15 and 16 were built by Siemens in 1891, while locomotive 17 is thought to have been built at Stockwell Depot along with numbers 21 and 22. Locomotives 18 and 23–52 were built by Crompton and Co. Number 19 was built by the Electric Construction Company and number 20 by Thames Ironworks.

The original 30 coaches, known as 'padded cells', were constructed by the Ashbury Carriage & Iron Company Ltd. More carriages were built by various manufacturers including GF Milnes and Co, Bristol Carriage & Wagon Co, Oldbury Carriage & Wagon Co, Hurst Nelson & Co, and the Brush Electrical Engineering Co, eventually collectively constructing 165 carriages. Later carriages had larger windows.

Trains originally consisted of one locomotive and three coaches, with a driver and two guards working each train. Four-coach trains were introduced when the line was extended to Clapham Common in June 1900. Trains were eventually extended to six carriages. The original rolling stock remained in service until the tunnels were rebuilt in 1924.

The City & South London Railway stock was replaced with 1923 Standard Stock.

City & South London Railway locomotive number 13, which was built by Mather & Platt Engineers for the opening of the railway in 1890. The locomotive is displayed at the London Transport Museum at Covent Garden and is seen here on 16 July 2022.

One of the original 'padded cells' built for the City & South London Railway. The carriages had small windows but very comfortable seats. Later carriages were provided with larger windows, partly to assist passengers with identifying the stations. Gates were provided at the end of the carriages in the years before power-operated doors were invented. This vehicle is number 30 and was built by the Ashbury Carriage and Iron Company. It is displayed alongside locomotive 13 at the London Transport Museum at Covent Garden, on 16 July 2022.

City & South London Railway carriage 163 was built by the Brush Electrical Engineering Co in 1907. It was one of the first carriages to be built from steel rather than wood. It is at the (now closed) Electric Railway Museum near Coventry on 14 May 2016. The carriage has since moved to London for repair. A second carriage, number 135, moved to a private location in Kent for eventual restoration.

The Charing Cross, Euston and Hampstead Railway (1906 Gate Stock)

The Charing Cross, Euston and Hampstead Railway ordered a fleet of 30 trains from the American Car and Foundry Company, which were manufactured in the US but assembled in Manchester. The 30 trains were made up of 150 carriages formed into five-car sets for the rush hour, and operating as two- or three-carriage sets during off-peak periods. Gates, operated by gatemen, were postioned at the end of each carriage, and were known as the 1906 Gate Stock. These were withdrawn on 31 January 1929 and replaced with the 1923 Standard Stock.

Although none of the Charing Cross, Euston and Hampstead Railway rolling stock survives, part of a Great Northern, Piccadilly and Brompton Railway (Piccadilly line) carriage number 51 has been restored and is displayed at the London Transport Depot at Acton, 14 September 2014.

A non-stop train formed of Gate Stock seen at Golders Green in 1911. (Copyright TfL from the London Transport Museum Collection)

1923–27 Stock and 1928–29 Stock (Standard Stock)

An initial order for 191 new carriages was split between three companies; Cammell Laird, The Metropolitan Carriage Works and Finance Company, and the Birmingham Railway Carriage & Wagon Company, following the successful testing of some prototype units built in 1922. There was a further order, in 1924, for 127 carriages, and another in 1925 for a further 120 carriages. The new trains were fitted with air-operated sliding doors. The final Northern line fleet consisted of 724 carriages formed into seven-carriage sets, with three- and four-carriage sets running at off-peak times.

The Standard Stock was later replaced by the 1938 Stock when deliveries commenced in 1938, although the Standard Stock was retained on the Northern City line until 1966 before being replaced by 1938 Stock.

A number of Standard Stock units saw service on the Isle of Wight between 1967 and 1990 (classified as Class 485 and 486), before being replaced by 1938 stock. A number of vehicles are preserved.

A pair of Standard Stock trains pass at Ryde Esplanade on 18 July 1987. The right-hand platform and running line have since been taken out of use.

A train of Standard Stock in Network SouthEast livery at Morden Depot on 11 November 1990, during the Tube Centenary celebrations.

A preserved Standard Stock car, carrying a Drayton Park destination plate, at the London Transport Depot Museum at Acton Town on 22 April 2018.

The 1938 Stock

Following the success of the experimental 1935 Stock, which was tested on the Piccadilly line, the 1938 Stock was ordered as part of the 1935–1940 New Works Programme. Some trains were jointly owned by the LNER and the fleet consisted of more than 1,100 carriages. Further vehicles were ordered in 1949 and some of the 1935 Stock cars were later converted to run with the 1938 Stock.

The 1938 Stock first entered service on the Northern line on 30 June 1938 and operated on it until 1978. Five sets of 1938 Stock were reintroduced between 1986 and 1988 to provide additional capacity, including the *Starlight Express* set, which was fully refurbished and named after the West End musical.

Several sets of 1938 Stock saw further life operating Island Line services on the Isle of Wight until 2021. Some carriages also moved to the preserved railway on Alderney, in the Channel Islands, but were replaced by 1959 Stock cars when they became life expired. Several units have been preserved on the Isle of Wight and at other locations around the country, including at the London Transport Museum.

Starlight Express 1938 Stock unit at Morden on 13 June 1987.

Preserved 1938 Stock unit, carrying Piccadilly line destination plates, at the London Transport Depot Museum at Acton Town on 14 September 2014.

A number of 1938 Stock units saw subsequent service on the Isle of Wight (replacing the Standard Stock that also found a new home on the island). The last 1938 Stock train operated in early 2021 and was replaced by former District line D Stock rolling stock (classified Class 484), which was also converted for operation on the island. This picture is of units 483008 and 483006 passing at Sandown on 19 October 2018.

A set of 1938 Stock (483004) remained on the Isle of Wight at Holliers Park near Arreton, following its replacement with former District line rolling stock, 31 December 2021. Unit 483007 has also been preserved on the island and is located at the Isle of Wight Steam Railway in Haven Street.

Nine-carriage trains

By the mid-1930s, Northern line overcrowding was becoming a problem at peak times. In 1936, proposals were drawn up to operate a number of nine-carriage trains between Edgware and Kennington via Charing Cross. The platforms at Burnt Oak, Colindale, Hendon Central, Brent Cross and Golders Green were extended to accommodate the longer train length, although most of the works were later removed. Minor changes were also made at Tottenham Court Road and Leicester Square. The turnback siding at Colindale was extended along with Platform 1 at Edgware, which was completed in 1938.

The Standard Stock was re-formed to provide some nine-car trains, the first of which was introduced on 8 November 1937 between Colindale and Kennington. During the morning rush-hour the last two carriages remained in the tunnel between Golders Green and Tottenham Court Road. At Tottenham Court Road, the front two carriages stopped in the tunnel, enabling passengers to leave from the rear two carriages. From Tottenham Court Road to Kennington, the rear two carriages remained in the tunnel again but by now were empty. In the evening rush hour, the front two carriages remained in the tunnel between Kennington and Leicester Square, so were not available for use. At Tottenham Court Road the front two carriages stopped in the platform, but then remained in the tunnel until reaching Golders Green.

Plans were drawn up to introduce more nine-car services and extend the platforms at Euston, Camden Town and Kennington, along with the introduction of nine-car trains on the Highgate branch. The Bank branch was excluded from the plans, as was the section between Kennington and Morden. Due to the onset of World War Two, nine-car trains were withdrawn in September 1939. With the exception of the Moorgate to Alexandra Palace route, the extensions planned as part of the 1935–1940 New Works Programme would have facilitated the introduction of nine-car trains. Only some of the work to enable nine-car operations was completed, including the new platforms at Highgate (low level) and the new station at East Finchley. The new

1938 Stock mainly consisted of seven-carriage trains (formed into three- and four-car sets), but ten nine-car trains, specifically ordered for peak-hour services between High Barnet/Edgware and Kennington via Charing Cross, were also constructed. A limited number of nine-car 1938 Stock trains commenced in June 1939 but were withdrawn by September that year and converted to seven-car sets.

The 1956 Stock

Three seven-car prototype 1956 Stock trains were constructed by different manufacturers, and were tested on the Piccadilly line. Following the successful trial, a large order for 1959 and the similar 1962 stock was placed, which was developed from the 1956 prototype trains. The 1956 Stock was transferred to the Northern line in 1976–77, where it remained until being withdrawn in 1995.

A train of 1956 Stock departing from Finchley Central for Mill Hill East, displaying an Edgware via Charing Cross destination blind, on 19 June 1987.

A train of 1956 Stock at East Finchley with a train from Morden in December 1986.

The 1959/1962 Stock

The 1959 Stock was built by Metro-Cammell and consisted of 76 seven-carriage trains. The trains first operated on the Northern line in 1975 and remained there until their final withdrawal in 2000. A few sets of 1962 Stock built as a follow-on order, mainly for the Central line, also operated on the Northern line before being withdrawn in 1999.

A row of 1959 Stock units at Morden Depot on 11 November 1990 during the Tube Centenary celebrations.

A train of 1959 Stock preparing to depart from Morden with a train for Edgware on 13 June 1987.

A 1959 Stock carriage 1030, displaying a Hampstead destination blind, at the Mangapps Farm Railway Museum near Burnham-on-Crough in Essex on 15 August 2020.

1959 rolling stock vehicles 1044 and 1045, displaying a Colindale destination blind, at Braye Road station on the island of Alderney on 19 August 2007. The 1959 Stock replaced a 1938 stock unit that operated on Alderney previously.

Car 1305 of 1959 Stock was displayed at the Sutton Hall Miniature Railway near Rochford in Essex for a number of years before moving to a private location in Cambridgeshire. This photograph was taken on 27 June 2014.

Car 1031 of 1959 Stock is preserved at the Epping and Ongar Railway in Essex and is seen here at North Weald on 29 December 2019. The Epping and Ongar Railway operates over a section of the former Central line, which closed on 30 September 1994.

The 1972 Stock

Sixty-three trains of 1972 Stock were built in two batches, known as Mark I and Mark II stock and were similar to 1967 Stock built for the Victoria line. The 1972 Mark I stock was originally ordered for the Northern line and consisted of 30 seven-carriage trains, entering service between June 1972 and June 1973.

The 33 trains of 1972 Mark II stock were ordered shortly afterwards and initially entered service on the Northern line in November 1973. Between 1977 and 1979, the 1972 Mark II stock was transferred to the Bakerloo line in readiness for the opening of the Jubilee line, which took over operation of the Stanmore branch of the Bakerloo line in 1979. A number of 1972 Mark II stock returned to the Northern line in 1983, with more units transferring in 1984 and 1985, following delivery of the 1983 stock to the Jubilee line. The 1972 Mark II stock moved to the Bakerloo line in 1987, while the 1972 Mark I stock remained in service on the Northern line until it was replaced by 1995 Stock in 1999. 1972 Stock still operates on the Bakerloo line today.

1972 Mark I stock units at Morden Depot on 11 November 1990 during the Tube Centenary celebrations.

1972 and 1959 Stock trains at Golders Green in August 1986.

A train of 1972 Mark II stock at High Barnet. The Mark II stock had red doors, while the Mark I units were unpainted. (Reg Batten)

The 1995 Stock

The 1995 Stock consisted of 106 six-carriage trains, which were manufactured by GEC Alstom. They entered service between 1998 and 2001 providing the Northern line with a single fleet of trains. A number of alterations were carried out to facilitate the introduction of the new trains including modification to the depots at Edgware, Golders Green, Highgate and Morden, and to the sidings at High Barnet. The new trains facilitated the conversion of the line to Automatic Train Operation (ATO) between 2013 and 2014. Between 2013 and 2015 the rolling stock was refurbished.

A train of 1995 Stock approaching Brent Cross on 29 January 2022.

A train of 1995 Stock at Brent Cross on 25 November 2022.

A line up of 1995 Stock at Morden Depot on 17 May 2015.

Chapter 8
Depots and Sidings

Aldenham Depot

Aldenham Depot would have replaced Golders Green as the principal maintenance facility for the line under the 1935–1940 New Works Programme proposals. Good progress was made with construction, which enabled the depot to be modified and used for aircraft construction during World War Two. After the war, once it became clear that the Northern line extension was not going to progress, the buildings were converted into a bus overhaul works, handling up to 50 vehicles a week.

In the 1970s, there were proposals to use Aldenham Works as a bus and rail overhaul depot. A new line was proposed to connect Aldenham Depot with Stanmore, and a station at Aldenham was also suggested as a possible option. Aldenham Bus Overhaul works closed in November 1986 and the building was demolished in 1996 to make way for an industrial estate.

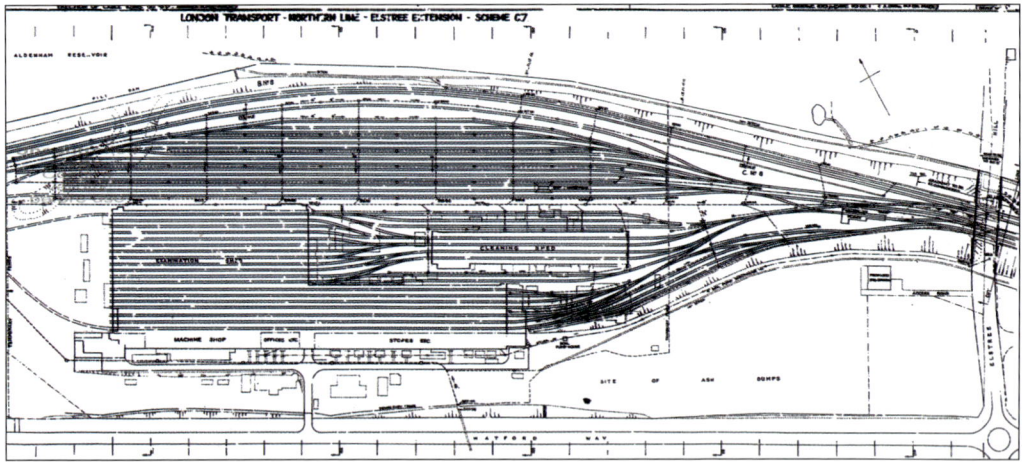

This plan shows the full extent of the depot at Aldenham. To the left of the drawing is the route towards Bushey Heath station, while on the right is the line towards Edgware. The Watford Way runs across the bottom of the drawing, parallel to the depot. Elstree Hill crosses the railway to the right-hand side of the plan, with a short service road leading to the proposed sub-station site. The depot consisted of stabling sidings, the large Examination Shed and a smaller four-road cleaning shed. The rooms at the bottom of the plan are the Machine Shop, Office and Stores. (Copyright TfL from the TfL Engineering Records Collection)

A view of Aldenham Bus Overhaul Works taken from the site entrance in summer 1986, shortly before closure.

A view of Aldenham Bus Overhaul Works, originally constructed as a depot for the Northern line, shortly after opening in 1956. (Copyright TfL from the London Transport Museum Collection)

Drayton Park Depot

Drayton Park Depot served the line from opening in 1904 and was modernised as part of the 1935–1940 New Works Programme. The depot remained in use as a maintenance location until 1966, after which it became a stabling location only. Rolling stock was then transferred elsewhere for maintenance. The site was closed when the route transferred to British Rail in 1975.

A view of Drayton Park Depot in September 1966, looking towards Moorgate. The station is on the left of the view. A train of Standard Stock, which is in the depot, was replaced by 1938 Stock shortly afterwards. (Copyright TfL from the London Transport Museum Collection)

Looking towards Finsbury Park from the adjacent road bridge, we see the overgrown site of Drayton Park Depot on 1 July 2017, after the depot buildings had been demolished.

Edgware Depot and Sidings

Edgware Depot originally consisted of a four-carriage shed alongside four open-air sidings. Additional sidings were due to be added as part of the 1935–1940 New Works Programme but the work was not completed. Two sidings were laid on the second route, towards Golders Green, and were partly constructed as part of the programme, but were later removed. To provide additional capacity for the 1995 rolling stock, seven additional sidings were provided at Edgware in 1996 (three for use by engineering trains).

Golders Green Depot

Golders Green Depot was opened by the Charing Cross, Euston and Hampstead Railway and was completed in March 1907. The site was extended to provide additional sidings on the depot site, as well as between the running lines. The shunt neck was extended into a blind tunnel mouth in 1923–24 to accommodate longer trains. The depot site has always been constrained, with access from the London direction only. Under the 1935–1940 New Works Programme, Aldenham Depot was due to replace Golders Green as the principal maintenance depot for the Northern line.

A line-up of Northern line rolling stock at Golders Green Depot on 16 January 1987, including 1959, 1972, 1938 and 1956 Stock.

A view of Golders Green Depot taken in 1933 looking towards Edgware. (Copyright TfL from the London Transport Museum Collection)

High Barnet Sidings

High Barnet Sidings were constructed as part of the 1935–1940 New Works Programme, when services were extended to High Barnet. The eight sidings eventually constructed were originally designed to accommodate nine-carriage trains. Trains were also regularly stabled in the platforms at High Barnet. Although only one shunt neck was provided, a second shunt neck was added as part of modifications undertaken to accommodate the 1995 Stock.

Highgate Depot and Highgate Wood Sidings

Highgate Wood Sidings were due to be reconstructed as part of the 1935–1940 New Works Programme. The existing four sidings were due to be replaced with six sidings and a reception road connected at both ends, providing direct access to the Alexandra Palace branch, as well as a connection towards Highgate via Park Junction. A number of maintenance sidings would also have been provided. The plans for Highgate Wood Sidings were revised to provide six electrified sidings connected at the Highgate end only, along with some maintenance sidings.

Highgate Depot replaced the previous Wellington Sidings and goods yard. Highgate Depot would have consisted of eight covered sidings and three open sidings, accessible from the north and the south, and a reception line.

There were plans to rebuild Highgate Depot due to the widening of the adjacent Archway Road (A1), which was proposed in the early 1970s but eventually dropped in 1990. Highgate Wood Sidings would have been removed and a second depot building constructed, containing seven sidings, alongside the existing depot building.

Highgate Depot was rebuilt in 1970 but closed on 25 March 1984 along with Park Junction Signal Box, which was demolished in 1995. Highgate Wood Sidings were closed in December 1982. Highgate Depot reopened on 23 January 1989, with the south exit opening in 1996 when the sidings were lengthened in preparation for the new 1995 Stock.

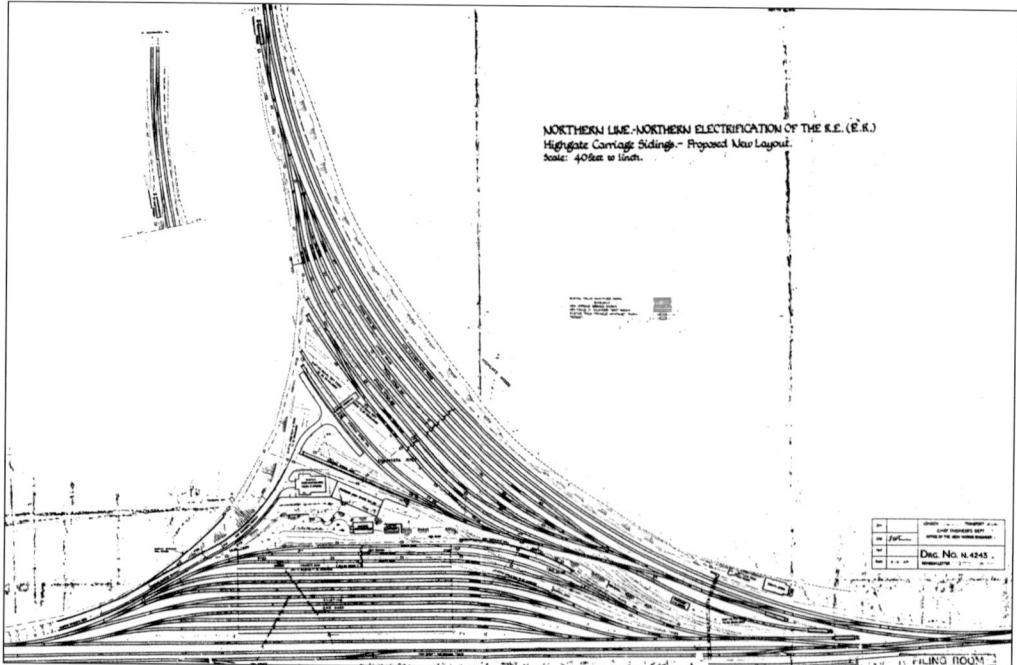

This plan shows Highgate Depot and Highgate Wood Sidings, adjacent to the Alexandra Palace branch. East Finchley is to the left, Highgate to the right and the Alexandra Palace branch curves away to the top of the drawing. (Copyright TfL from the TfL Engineering Records Collection)

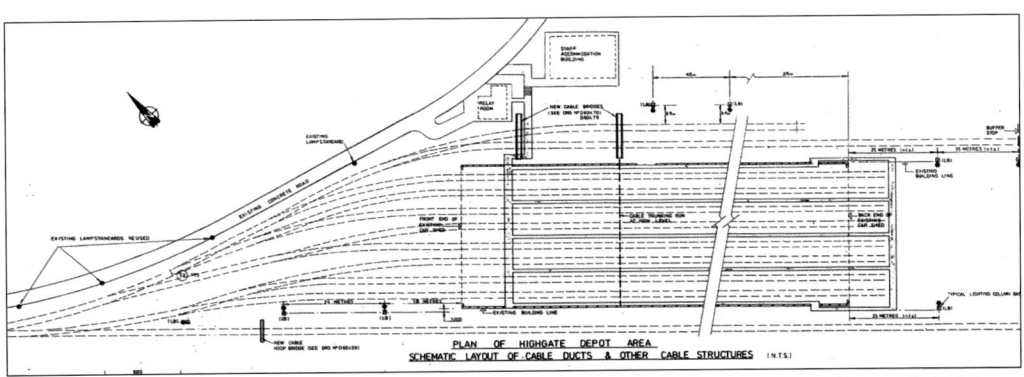

PLAN OF HIGHGATE DEPOT AREA
SCHEMATIC LAYOUT OF CABLE DUCTS & OTHER CABLE STRUCTURES [N.T.S.]

This plan, dated March 1988, was drawn up ahead of Highgate Depot reopening in 1989. (Copyright TfL from the TfL Engineering Records Collection)

This drawing was produced in 1995 and shows the depot layout with both north and south exits open. (Copyright TfL from the TfL Engineering Records Collection)

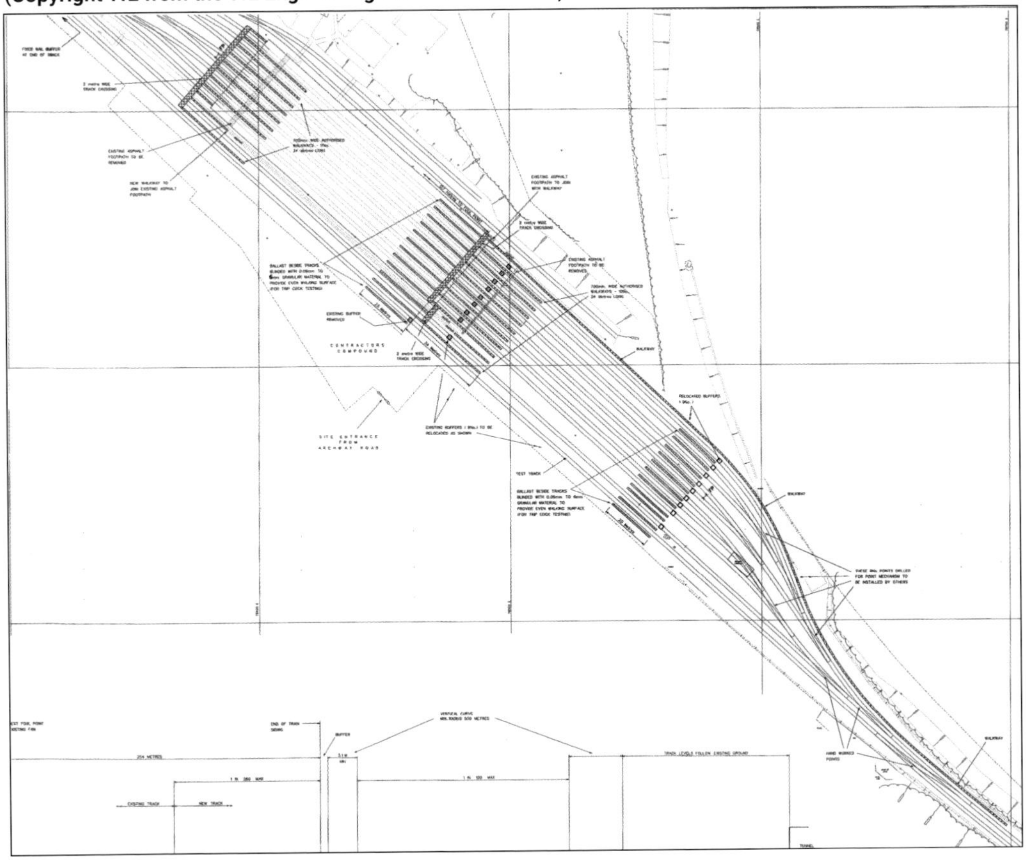

Highgate Wood Sidings in November 1986, four years after they had been taken out of use.

Highgate Depot in November 1986. In the years before closure, only the north exit was in use. At this time, the depot was not in use, but reopened in 1989.

Highgate Depot on 23 January 2016 with one train of 1995 Stock stabled at the Highgate end of the site.

Morden Depot

Morden Depot opened in 1926 when the Morden extension opened, and consisted of a shed as well as a number of open-air sidings. The depot has two reception roads, both provided with carriage washers, and received some modifications to accommodate the 1995 Stock.

The interior of Morden Depot on 11 November 1990 during the Tube Centenary celebrations.

There is a long footbridge that crosses Morden Depot, which offers excellent views of the depot. This photograph, taken in December 1986, includes 1972, 1938 and 1959 rolling stock.

A view of Morden Depot taken on 17 May 2015, following modernisation for the 1995 Stock. The smaller paint-shop building can be seen to the right of road 25.

Stockwell Depot

Stockwell Depot was opened by the City & South London Railway in 1890 and housed the power station as well as rolling-stock maintenance and stabling facilities. Originally the depot was connected to the tunnels by a steep ramp, but this was replaced by a lift in 1907. The power station closed in 1915, followed by the depot itself in 1923, although it was used for engineering trains for a few more years. The depot site was always congested and was modified a number of times to make best use of the space. Nothing remains of the depot today, other than some of the underground tunnels that once connected the running lines to the depot.

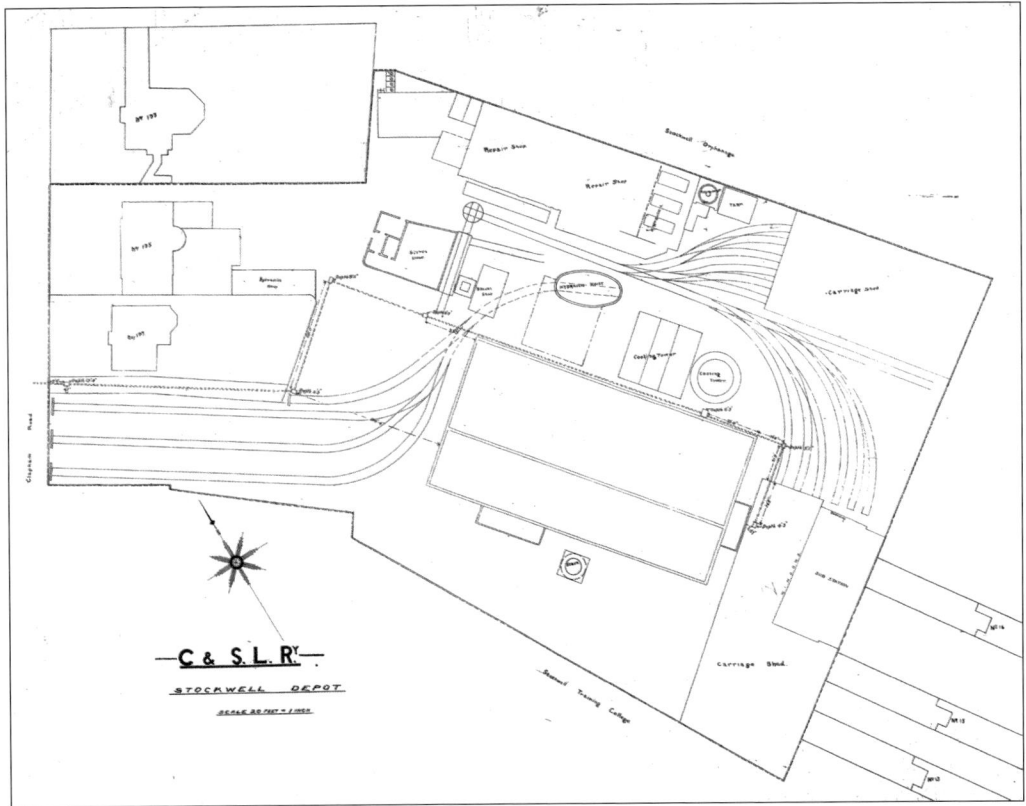

A plan of Stockwell Depot, showing the hoist that was used to transfer rolling stock to and from the tunnels, and which replaced the original ramp. The compact nature of the site can be seen, including two carriage sheds and sidings. (Copyright TfL from the TfL Engineering Records Collection)

Locomotive number 36 with carriage number 10 at Stockwell Depot in June 1925. (Copyright TfL from the London Transport Museum Collection)

A Mather & Platt maker's plate fitted to City & South London Railway locomotive number 13, which is displayed at the London Transport Museum, Covent Garden, 16 July 2022.

Chapter 9
Stations

The Northern line stations have a variety of architectural styles. The oldest ones date from 1867 and were built by the Great Northern Railway, while more modern architecture can be seen at Tottenham Court Road, which was recently modernised and expanded to incorporate the Elizabeth line, which opened on 24 May 2022. It is still possible to find some original City & South London Railway stations, as well as buildings designed by famous London Transport architects Leslie Green, Stanley Heaps and Charles Holden.

The entrance to Clapham North station on 3 December 2022. The building was reconstructed in the 1920s by the well known London Transport architect Charles Holden.

Hampstead station is one of the deepest on the Underground system and was originally going to be called Heath Street. The station was designed by Leslie Green and still retains lifts between the surface and the platforms, 29 January 2022.

High Barnet was originally opened by the Great Northern Railway on 1 April 1872. The station buildings were due to be replaced as part of the 1935–1940 New Works Programme, but the work was not progressed. The station has three platforms and retains a number of heritage features, 8 August 2021.

Clapham North on 3 December 2022. A number of stations originally consisted of island platforms including Euston, Angel and Clapham Common. Angel and Euston have since been rebuilt, leaving just Clapham Common and Clapham North with narrow island platforms.

Oval station on 8 August 2021. Oval station originally opened as The Oval but was renamed a few years after opening. The station was refurbished in 1998.

Kennington station on 8 August 2021. Kennington is the best preserved of the original City & South London Railway stations and retains the distinctive dome that houses the lift mechanism. The lift was originally hydraulic but was replaced with an electric lift in 1897.

Edgware station, which was designed by Stanley Heaps, was opened on 18 August 1924. Some changes were made to the buildings as part of the 1935–1940 New Works Programme.

The surface-level building at Mornington Crescent is a fine example of a Leslie Green station, 7 February 2016.

Mornington Crescent was closed in 1992 to enable the lifts to be replaced, but due to funding issues it remained closed until 1998. A northbound train arrives on 3 December 2022.

Many of the underground stations are still served by lifts, including Belsize Park, which has four lifts in operation. The platform-level lift entrance on 3 December 2022.

The grand surface-level station building at Belsize Park, another Leslie Green design, on 3 December 2022.

Original tiling can still be seen at many stations, including Chalk Farm, 3 December 2022.

Mill Hill East station was opened as Mill Hill by the Great Northern Railway on 22 August 1867. The original building remains, 23 July 2022.

Finchley Central station was opened on 22 August 1867 by the Great Northern Railway. It was originally named Finchley and Hendon, and was later renamed Finchley, and then Finchley Church End. The station became Finchley Central when Northern line services commenced in April 1940. The station was due to be rebuilt with four platforms as part of the 1935–1940 New Works Programme, but the work was cancelled, meaning that many of the original station buildings remain today, 23 July 2022.

Golders Green has three tracks and five platforms, although Platform 1 is for staff access only. This view is of a 1938 Stock unit preparing to depart for central London in December 1986.

The surface-level building at Chalk Farm, designed by Leslie Green, on 3 December 2022.

The distinctive tiling by the artist Eduardo Paolozzi at Tottenham Court Road on 3 December 2022.

Woodside Park was originally opened by the Great Northern Railway as Torrington Park on 1 April 1872. It was renamed Torrington Park, Woodside before becoming Woodside Park in 1882. This is one of two former GNR signal boxes at Woodside Park, but it is no longer in use, 8 August 2021.

Northbound Platform 1 at Totteridge and Whetstone on 8 August 2021. The station was opened as Totteridge by the Great Northern Railway on 1 April 1872, being renamed Totteridge and Whetstone two years later. The station retains many original GNR features.

West Finchley was opened by the London & North Eastern Railway (LNER) on 1 March 1933, with Northern line services commencing on 14 April 1940. This is the northbound Platform 1, on 8 August 2021.

The original station building at Morden, designed by Charles Holden and finished using Portland stone, was supplemented by an office building in the 1960s. The station remains an important bus interchange, 17 May 2015.

Chapter 10

Recent Developments

Light railway proposals
The Muswell Hill Metro Group has long campaigned to reopen the line between Alexandra Palace and Finsbury Park, with stations at or near their original locations at Alexandra Palace, Muswell Hill, Cranley Gardens, Highgate (high level), Crouch End, Stroud Green, and Finsbury Park. Most of the route is still intact, apart from a couple of short sections, currently in use as a parkland walk. The Muswell Hill Metro Group has suggested that the line is reopened as a light railway or tramway to reduce construction costs. This would potentially enable the parkland walk to share the route of the light railway.

London Regional Transport published a report called *Light Rail for London?* in 1986, which considered options for new light rail systems. A number of routes were considered, which fell into three categories:

Category 1 Conversion of existing rail routes with or without possible extension.
Category 2 New routes to serve inner and outer London developments.
Category 3 Conversion of major bus corridors.

Category 1
One of the options considered was conversion of the Northern line to light rail between Finchley Central and High Barnet, and between Finchley Central and Mill Hill East with a possible extension to Mill Hill (Broadway) and Edgware. The scheme was given a low priority.

Category 2
Consideration was given to reopening the line between Alexandra Palace and Highgate as a light rail route, with an extension from Alexandra Palace to Wood Green along existing streets or as a segregated route. It, too, was given a low priority. The report eventually led to the development of the Croydon Tramlink network.

St Helier extension
The *Railways for London* report, published by the Campaign to Improve London's Transport, advocated a single-track extension of the Northern line from Morden to St Helier to provide a connection with the national rail network, with the potential for Northern line trains to continue to Sutton Common.

The Croydon Tramlink network has been very successful. Tram 2543, built by Bombardier, is at Therapia Lane on 21 July 2019. The tram network serves Morden Road, which is a short walk from Morden station.

RAIL STUDIES
The 1974 *London Rail Study*

The *London Rail Study* (also known as the *Barran Report* after Sir David Barran, who led the study) was published in November 1974. The remit was '... to review the arrangements for passenger travel by rail wholly or mainly within Greater London... and possible options for the provision and modification of services to meet future needs...'.

The *London Rail Study* only made brief reference to the Northern line, noting that passenger numbers had declined between Golders Green and Edgware (probably due to the ageing population), but there was still peak-hour overcrowding on many sections of the line. At this time, Stage One of the Fleet line (later renamed the Jubilee line) was in progress between Baker Street and Charing Cross, including modifications to Strand station, which was being remodelled to create a Northern, Bakerloo and Fleet line interchange. It was recommended that Stage Two of the Fleet line should be progressed from Charing Cross to Fenchurch Street. The Ring Rail scheme, which was a proposed London orbital railway, was also discussed (elements of which have since been delivered as part of the London Overground network), but the option of diverting the Northern line to provide an improved connection at Camden Town was discounted. Improvements to interchange arrangements at King's Cross were also proposed.

LUL Strategic Review/South London Access Study 1988

London Underground Ltd initially considered four options for extending the Northern line beyond Kennington:

Route A Kennington to Streatham via Brixton, Brixton Hill and Streatham Hill.
Route B Kennington to Peckham Rye via Camberwell Green.
Route C Kennington to Tulse Hill via Camberwell Green, Denmark Hill and Herne Hill.
Route D Kennington to Balham utilising the deep-level shelters.

Routes C and D were discounted, but Routes A and B were put forward in 1988–89 as part of the *South London Access Study*. Minor works would also have been required at Camden Town and Kennington plus additional stabling, probably at Highgate (Wood Sidings).

There was a further proposal in 1992 to extend the Northern line from Kennington to Streatham and perhaps onwards to Croydon. An alternative option put forward was for an extension from Kennington to Crystal Palace via Camberwell and Brockwell Park.

The Central London Rail Study 1989

The *Central London Rail Study* was published in January 1989 and considered a number of options for upgrading the main line and underground network, including several new lines and extensions. It mentioned splitting the Northern line into two separate lines to improve performance and increase capacity mainly due to the constraints at Kennington. The line would be split into a Morden via Bank, and a Kennington via Charing Cross service, removing direct trains from Morden via Charing Cross.

The Railway Development Society suggested construction of additional reversing facilities at Kennington, or extending the Charing Cross branch from Kennington towards Streatham, Tulse Hill or Peckham Rye as an alternative.

Transport 2025

In 2006, Transport for London published its 2025 strategy document. Segregating the Northern line was considered, enabling 30 trains per hour in each direction to operate on both the Bank and Charing Cross branches. Station capacity works would have been required at Camden Town to facilitate interchange between the Bank and Charing Cross branches. Additional rolling stock and stabling would also be required.

STATION PROJECTS
Angel

By the mid-1980s, Angel station was becoming increasingly overcrowded. The station retained lifts and a narrow island platform, originally provided by the City & South London Railway in 1901. Funding was secured to reconstruct the station with escalators and a new northbound tunnel and platform, enabling the existing southbound platform to be widened across the former northbound platform. The original station entrance on Torrens Street was closed and replaced with a new entrance on Islington High Street, which opened in autumn 1992. At the same time, the lifts were replaced by some of the longest escalators on the underground.

The southbound platform at Angel on 29 January 2022, following rebuilding. This tunnel originally contained the northbound and southbound lines and a narrow island platform.

The original Angel station entrance on Torrens Street on 29 January 2022.

Bank

Bank station had become increasingly congested, so plans were drawn up for a significant upgrade project. Work commenced in April 2016 and is due to be completed in mid-2023. The works included the construction of a new southbound Northern line tunnel and platform, enabling the former southbound platform to be used for a larger underground concourse and other improvements. The Northern line was closed between Kennington and Moorgate from 15 January to 15 May 2022 to enable the new tunnel to be connected. Two new lifts, two moving walkways and 12 new escalators are being installed. Two new entrances have been provided, the first on Walbrook, which opened in November 2018, and the second entrance on Cannon Street which opened in February 2023.

The new Bank station entrance on Cannon Street under construction on 11 June 2021.

The new Bank station entrance on Walbrook on 17 July 2021.

Charing Cross

Major works were undertaken in conjunction with the Fleet line (later renamed Jubilee line) extension from Baker Street to Charing Cross. Strand station (on the Northern line) and Trafalgar Square station (on the Bakerloo line) were reconstructed, reopening as a combined station called Charing Cross station serving all three lines. The Jubilee line extension to Charing Cross was the first stage of a proposed route towards Fenchurch Street and south-east London. The Jubilee line platforms at Charing Cross were closed on 19 November 1999, when the Jubilee line was extended through to Stratford via Canary Wharf following a different alignment.

Euston

Euston station was reconstructed in the 1960s to provide an interchange with the Victoria line. The northbound line on the Bank branch was diverted on a new alignment, with a new northbound platform providing a cross-platform interchange with the northbound Victoria line. The former island platform, constructed by the City & South London Railway in 1907, continued to be used by the southbound Northern line, but the former northbound trackbed was built over to provide a wide platform and interchange with the southbound Victoria line. A crossover was retained at the King's Cross end of the station.

London Bridge

London Bridge station was reconstructed as part of the Jubilee line extension to Stratford. A new southbound Northern line tunnel and platform were opened in 1996, enabling the former southbound platform to be turned into a pedestrian concourse between the northbound and southbound lines. New interchange tunnels were built to connect with the Jubilee line and the main line station.

There have been further changes to the station at surface level in recent years as a result of the Thameslink Project and construction of the adjacent Shard skyscraper.

Old Street

Old Street station originally opened on 17 November 1901 and has changed several times since; it was rebuilt in 1925 and again in 1968 when the surface buildings were removed. Further works took place in 2014, and improvements are currently in progress.

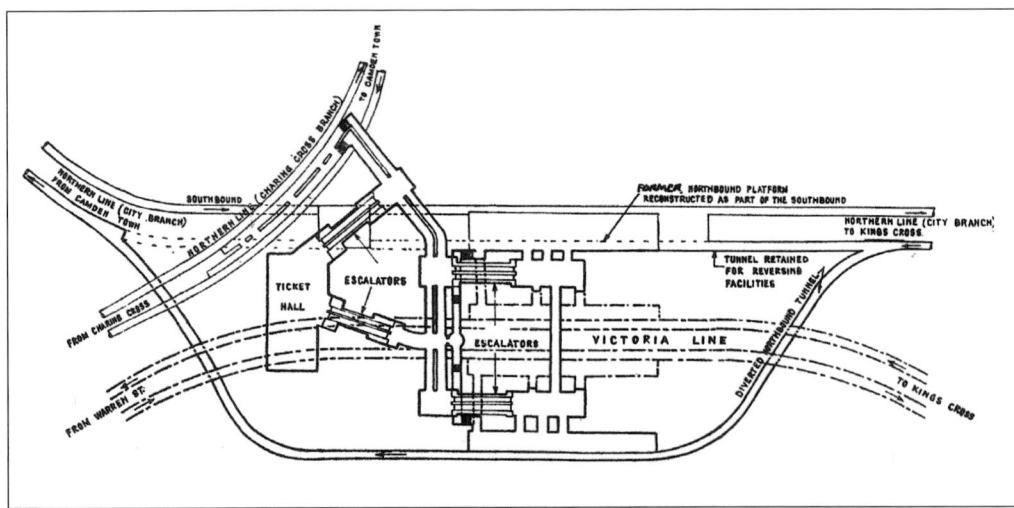

A plan of Euston station, showing the diverted northbound Northern line Bank Branch tunnel, and the cross-platform interchange provided between the Northern line (Bank Branch) and the Victoria line, as well as the connection to the Northern line Charing Cross branch. (Copyright TfL from the TfL Engineering Records Collection)

Tottenham Court Road

A number of changes have been made to Tottenham Court Road including refurbishment in 1984. More recently, major works were undertaken as part of the Crossrail project, with Elizabeth line trains introduced from 24 May 2022.

Warren Street

The station has been modified a number of times including the Victoria line interchange, which opened in 1968.

Waterloo

A number of changes were made at Waterloo in preparation for the Jubilee line extension in the late 1990s.

Copthall Stadium extension

In 1990, proposals were made to extend the Mill Hill East Branch towards Copthall (around 1.3km), including a second platform at Mill Hill East.

The Battersea extension

A number of options were considered including a route via Vauxhall to Battersea, before the extension via Nine Elms to Battersea Power Station was confirmed. Construction work commenced in 2015, with some of the £1.1bn cost being funded by the developers of Battersea Power Station. The railway is two miles long and branches off the Kennington loop. There are two stations, at Nine Elms and Battersea Power Station, both of which have two platforms. Passenger services commenced on 20 September 2021.

A southbound train heading for Battersea Power Station at Nine Elms on 23 September 2021, a few days after opening.

Nine Elms station under construction on 8 August 2020. The station serves the new American Embassy and other new developments taking place in the area.

The new Battersea Power Station station on 23 September 2021, a few days after opening. The station serves the Battersea Power Station development; a second entrance will be opened at a later date.

Chapter 11

Future Plans

Muswell Hill Metro
Much of the route between Finsbury Park and Alexandra Palace remains as a parkland walk, although a few buildings have been built on the trackbed. The Muswell Hill Metro Group campaigns for the line to be reopened as a light railway or tramway, although it seems unlikely that any progress will be made in the near future.

Clapham Junction extension
The Battersea Power Station extension has been designed to accommodate a further extension to Clapham Junction. This would complement the proposed Crossrail 2 project which would also serve Clapham Junction if progressed.

Splitting the Northern line
There are still longer-term aspirations to split the Northern line into two lines (one via Bank and one via Charing Cross), perhaps aligned with an extension to Clapham Junction and a remodelling of Camden Town to provide the necessary additional capacity.

Camden Town rebuilding
Camden Town station, as well as being an interchange station, also serves the nearby Camden Market and London Zoo. The station is often restricted to 'exit only' at weekends. There are proposals to rebuild the station to increase capacity, but budget constraints have prevented these from progressing.

The expansion of Bank station was completed in spring 2023. This is one of the new passageways.

Opening and Closure Dates

Northern Line opening dates

Section	Opened	Comments
King William Street to Stockwell	18 December 1890	Official opening 4 November 1890. Public service commenced 18 December 1890.
Borough to Moorgate Street	25 February 1900	Spur to King William Street closed at the same time.
Stockwell to Clapham Common	3 June 1900	Moorgate Street–Clapham Common closed between 29 November 1923 and 1 December 1924 for rebuilding.
Moorgate Street to Angel	17 November 1901	Moorgate Street–Euston closed between 9 August 1922 and 20 April 1924 for rebuilding.
Angel to Euston	12 May 1907	
Euston to Camden Town	20 April 1924	
Charing Cross to Golders Green / Archway	22 June 1907	
Charing Cross to Embankment	6 April 1914	
Golders Green to Hendon Central	19 November 1923	
Hendon Central to Edgware	18 August 1924	
Clapham Common to Morden	13 November 1926	
Kennington to Embankment	13 November 1926	
Archway to East Finchley	03 July 1939	Highgate (low level) opened 19 January 1941.
East Finchley to High Barnet	14 August 1940	Originally opened by the Great Northern Railway.
Finchley Central to Mill Hill East	18 May 1941	Originally opened by the Great Northern Railway.
Kennington to Battersea Power Station	20 November 2021	

* Short term closures are not shown.

Northern Line closure dates

Route / Station	Closed	Comments
King William Street to London Bridge	24 February 1900	

Northern City line opening dates

Route / Station	Opened	Comments
Finsbury Park to Moorgate	14 February 1904	Originally opened by the Great Northern & City Railway. Operated as part of the Metropolitan line from 1913 to 1939. Operated as part of the Northern line from 1939 until 1975. British Rail operation commenced in 1976.

Northern City line closure dates

Route / Station	Closed	Comments
Finsbury Park to Drayton Park	3 October 1964	The tunnels at Finsbury Park were subsequently used for the southbound Victoria line and southbound Piccadilly line platforms.
Moorgate to Drayton Park	5 October 1975	British Rail operation commenced in 1976.

* Short-term closures are not shown.

Station Names

Original Station Name	Subsequent Station Name	Current / Final Station Name	Notes
Agar Street		King William Street	Agar Street was proposed prior to opening.
Aldenham		Bushey Heath	Proposed station on the Elstree extension. Originally referred to as Aldenham, but later changed to Bushey Heath. A number of other proposals were put forward including South Aldenham, Bushey Heath & Aldenham, and Bushey & Aldenham.
Battersea		Battersea Power Station	Early plans referred to the station as Battersea.
Brent		Brent Cross	Renamed on 20 July 1976. Woodstock was also suggested prior to opening.
Burnt Oak	Burnt Oak (Watling)	Burnt Oak	Renamed Burnt Oak (Watling) in 1928 but the suffix has since been dropped. Sheaves Hill, Orange Hill, and Deansbrook were also suggested prior to opening.
Camden	Hampstead Road Camden (Mother Redcap)	Camden Town	These were the original names considered for a station in Camden. The site was later moved further north and the station was opened as Camden Town.
Castle Road		South Kentish Town	Referred to as Castle Road on early drawings. Some platform tiling was installed showing Castle Road.
Charing Cross	Charing Cross (Strand) Strand	Charing Cross	Renamed Charing Cross (Strand) on 6 April 1914. Renamed Strand on 9 May 1915. Renamed Charing Cross on 1 May 1979 after a period of closure during the construction of the Jubilee line.
Charing Cross (Embankment)	Charing Cross Charing Cross (Embankment)	Embankment	Renamed Charing Cross on 9 May 1915. Renamed Charing Cross Embankment on 4 August 1974. Renamed Embankment on 12 September 1976.
Clapham Road		Clapham North	Renamed on 13 September 1926.
Edgwarebury		Brockley Hill	Proposed station on the Elstree extension. A number of other proposals were also put forward including Edgebury, Canons, All Souls and North Edgware.

Original Station Name	Subsequent Station Name	Current / Final Station Name	Notes
Elstree or Elstree Hill		Elstree South	Proposed station on the Elstree extension.

Essex Road	Canonbury & Essex Road	Essex Road	Renamed Canonbury & Essex Road on 20 July 1922 while part of the Metropolitan line.
			    Renamed Essex Road on 11 July 1948, while part of the Northern line.
			    Now operated by National Rail (Great Northern).

Euston Road		Warren Street	Renamed on 7 June 1908. Euston Road tiling can still be seen.
Heath Street		Hampstead	Proposed name before opening, but some wall tiles were installed showing Heath Street, which can still be seen.
Highbury		Highbury & Islington	Renamed Highbury & Islington on 20 July 1922 while part of the Metropolitan line. Now operated by National Rail (Great Northern).

Highgate	Archway (Highgate)	Archway	Renamed Archway (Highgate) on 11 June 1939.
			    Highgate South was also considered, with Highgate called Highgate North or Highgate Wood.
			    Renamed Archway in December 1947.

Highgate North or Highgate Wood		Highgate	Highgate North or Highgate Wood also considered.
King's Cross for St Pancras		King's Cross St Pancras	Renamed King's Cross St Pancras in 1933.
Mill Hill East	Bittacy Hill	Mill Hill East	Bittacy Hill proposed to replace Mill Hill East.
Mill Hill The Hale	Mill Hill	Mill Hill The Hale	Mill Hill proposed to replace Mill Hill The Hale
Moorgate Street		Moorgate	Renamed Moorgate on 20 April 1924.
North Morden		Morden	Referred to as North Morden on early plans.
Nightingale Lane		Clapham South	Proposed name before opening.
North End	'Bull and Bush'	North End	Proposed station on Hampstead Heath. Partly constructed. Officially called North End, but often referred to unofficially as Bull & Bush after the nearby public house.
Oxford Street		Tottenham Court Road	Renamed Tottenham Court Road on 9 March 1908.
Seymour Street		Mornington Crescent	Proposed name before opening.

Original Station Name	Subsequent Station Name	Current / Final Station Name	Notes
South Wimbledon	South Wimbledon (Merton)	South Wimbledon	Renamed South Wimbledon (Merton) in 1928 but the suffix has since been dropped.
The Oval		Oval	Renamed in 1894.
Tottenham Court Road		Goodge Street	Renamed Goodge Street on 9 March 1908.
Trinity Road (Tooting Bec)		Tooting Bec	Renamed Tooting Bec on 1 October 1950.

A number of stations had alternative names before Northern line services were introduced, for example Finchley Central was called Finchley North End.

Warren Street station was originally called Euston Road, but was renamed shortly after opening in 1908. The original station name lives on in the historic tiling, which can still be seen today. This photograph was taken on 23 July 2022.

Hampstead station was originally going to be called Heath Street, but the name was changed shortly before opening. By that time tiling was in place and remains to this day. This photograph was taken on 29 January 2022.

In 1987, the original Clapham Road station sign was uncovered for a short while, more than 60 years after the station was renamed Clapham North. This photograph was taken on 7 June 1987.

Appendix C
A Selection of Tickets

Above left, above right and below: A selection of Northern line tickets. These are largely a thing of the past, as most journeys are now made using an Oyster Card or by contactless payment.

References and Further Reading

Books and booklets

A History of London Transport – Volume One, T C Baker and Michael Robbins, George Allen & Unwin Ltd, 1963

A History of London Transport – Volume Two, T C Baker and Michael Robbins, George Allen & Unwin Ltd, 1974

A to Z of London Underground Stations, Jason Cross, Train Crazy Publishing, 2019

Aldenham Works, A A M Durrant, London Transport

Ally Pally, C T Goode, Forge Books, 1983

By Tube Beyond Edgware, Tony Beard, Capital Transport, 2002

City & South London Railway – Reopening December 1924 (reprint), West Farthing Grange, 1990

The City & South London Railway, T S Lascelles, The Oakwood Press, 1987

Early Tube Railways of London, Nigel Pennick, Electric Traction Publications, 1983

Fifty Years of the Hampstead Tube, Charles E Lee, London Transport, 1957

Finsbury Park to Alexandra Palace, J E Connor, Middleton Press, 1997

London Rail – A Guide to TfL's Depots and Stabling Points, Paul Jordan and Paul Smith, Crecy Publishing Ltd, 2015

London's Disused Underground Stations, J E Connor, Capital Transport, 2021

London's Early Tube Railways, Nigel Pennick, Valknut Productions, 1988

London's Lost Railways, Charles Klapper, Routledge & Kegan Paul, 1976

London's Lost Tube Schemes, Antony Badsey-Ellis, Capital Transport, 2005

London Underground Rolling Stock, Brian Hardy, Capital Transport, various editions

London Underground Rolling Stock Guide (ABC), Ben Muldoon, Ian Allan, 2014

London Rail – a Guide to TfL's Depots and Stabling Points, Paul Jordan and Paul Smith, Crecy Publishing Ltd, 2015

London's Secret Tubes, Andrew Emmerson and Tony Beard, Capital Transport, 2004

London Transport Railways Handbook, Gregory D Beecroft, Iain D O Frew, Alan Holmewood, Barry Rayner and Barry Stevenson, The Foxley Press, 1983

London Transport Scrapbook, James Whiting, Capital Transport, various issues, 1975 to 1980

London's Underground – A Pictorial Survey, O J Morris, Ian Allan, 1950

London's Underground, John Glover, Railway World Special, 1984

London's Underground, John Glover, Ian Allan, various editions

Lost Underground Stations, John Glover, Crecy Publishing Ltd, 2014

Northern Line Extensions, Simon Murphy, Tempus Publishing Ltd, 2005

Northern Wastes, Jim Blake and Jonathan James, Platform Ten Productions/LPTL, 1987

Rails Through the Clay, D F Croome and Alan A Jackson, Capital Transport, 1993

Rails to the People's Palace, Reg Davies, Hornsey Historical Society, 1994

Secret Underground London, Nick Catford, Folly Books, 2013

The 1938 Tube Stock, Piers Connor, Capital Transport, 1989

The Amazing Electric Tube, Printz P Holman, London Transport Museum, 1990

The Big Tube, J Graeme Bruce, London Transport, 1976

The First Tube, Mike Horne and Bob Bayman, Capital Transport, 1990

The Hampstead Tube, Antony Badsey-Ellis, Capital Transport, 2007
The London Underground, Andrew Emmerson, Shire Publications, 2010
The London Underground Tube Stock, J Graeme Bruce, Ian Allan, 1988
The London Underground – An Illustrated History, Oliver Green, Ian Allan, 1987
The Northern line Extensions, Brian Hardy and MRFS, London Underground Railway Society, 2011
The Railway in Finchley, G F A Wilmot, Finchley Public Libraries Committee, 1962
The Railway in Finchley – Revised Edition, George Wilmot, Barnet London Borough Council, 1973
The Railway to King William Street, Peter Bancroft, 1981
The Shelter of the Tubes, John Gregg, Capital Transport, 2001
Tube Centenary 1890–1990 Souvenir Brochure, Northern Line, 1990
Tunnels Under London, Nigel Pennick, Electric Traction Publications, 1981
Underground Number 9 – The Northern line Extensions, Brian Hardy, London Underground Railway Society, 1981
Wimbledon's Railways, Alan Elliot, The Wimbledon Society, 1982

Reports
County of London Plan, J H Forshaw and P Abercrombie, London County Council, 1943
Light Rail for London, London Regional Transport, 1986
London Plan Working Party – Report to the Minister of Transport, British Transport Commission, 1949
LUL Strategic Review, D R Mead, London Underground Ltd, 1988
Railway (London Plan) Committee 1944 – Report to the Minister of War Transport, Ministry of Transport, 1946
Railway (London Plan) Committee 1944 – Final Report to the Minister of Transport, Ministry of Transport, 1948
Railways for London, Peter Kay, Campaign to Improve London's Transport
The Central London Rail Study, Department of Transport, 1989
The London Rail Study – Part 1 & Part 2 (The 'Barran Report'), Greater London Council / Department of the Environment, 1974
Transport 2025, Transport for London, 2006

Articles in *The London Railway Record* quarterly magazine
Published by Connor & Butler
The Alexandra Palace Line, J Derrick, No 6, January 1996
Tracing the Line to Alexandra Palace, Ian Baker, No 7, April 1996
Tracing the Mill Hill to Edgware Line, Ian Baker, No 10, January 1997
Over and Under in London, Michael J Smith, No 23, April 2000
A Notable Anniversary, No 23, April 2000
The Northern line Elstree Extension, Jonathan James No 23, April 2000
Northern line Extensions South of the River, Jonathan James, No 25, October 2000
Centenary of the Hampstead Tube, No 52, July 2017
Underground Non-Stop, Michael J Smith, No 57, October 2008
Ally Pally Farewell, J E Connor, No 57, October 2008
The Alexandra Palace, Edgware & High Barnet Lines – Some Ticket Aspects (Part One), Brian Pask, No 59, April 2009
The Alexandra Palace, Edgware & High Barnet Lines – Some Ticket Aspects (Part Two), Brian Pask, No 60, July 2009
Horror on the Hampstead Tube, Michael J Smith, No 61, October 2009
The London Plan, Jonathan James, No 65, October 2010
More on the Edgware Branch, Alan Lawrence, No 65, October 2010

Northern City Line Stock Transfers, John Collins, No 66, January 2011
North End (Bull & Bush), Nick Catford, Peter Kay, Peter Butler, No 74, January 2013
The Central London Rail Study 1988/89, Jonathan James, No 80, July 2014
Departing from Drayton Park, Roland Hummerston, S A Bawden, No 89, October 2016

Magazines
The City and South London Electric Railway, P V McMahon, *Cassier's Magazine*, Vol. XVI, No 4, August 1899
The City & South London Railway, *Railway World*, Ian Allan, December 1960
The First Railway to Edgware, A M Lawrence, *Railway World*, Ian Allan, September 1967
The Railway Battle of Barnet, A M Lawrence, *Railway World*, Ian Allan, May 1972
Closed Underground Stations, Edward Treby, *Railway World*, Ian Allan, May 1974
Bringing Back The Red, Michael Harris, *Railway World*, Ian Allan, February 1987
The Railway Gazette – Improving London's Transport, *The Railway Gazette*, May 1946
Jubilee of the City Tube, *Railway Magazine*, May 1941
The Wimbledon & Sutton Railway, Alan A Jackson, *Railway Magazine*, December 1966
Beyond Edgware, Alan A Jackson, *Railway Magazine*, February 1967
Almost a Tube, Part One, Alan A Jackson, *Railway Magazine*, May 1973
Almost a Tube, Part Two, Alan A Jackson, *Railway Magazine*, June 1973
Hertfordshire–Moorgate by Electric, *Railway Magazine*, August 1976
London's Railway Plan – *London Transport Magazine*, London Transport, Vol. 3, No 5, August 1949
Underground News, London Underground Railway Society

Maps
The London Underground – A Diagrammatic History (map), Douglas Rose, Capital Transport, various editions
London Transport Railway Track Map, John Yonge and Trevor Haynes, Quail Map Co, 1981

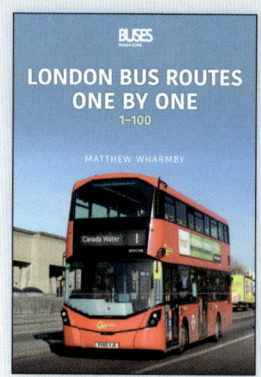
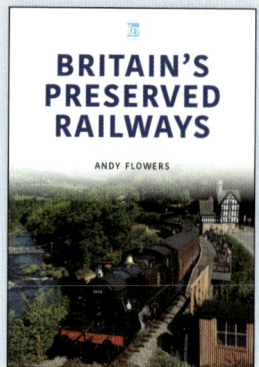
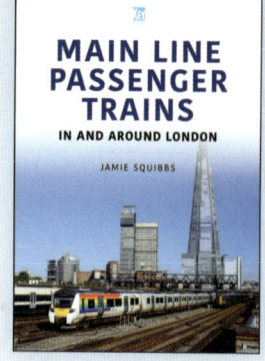
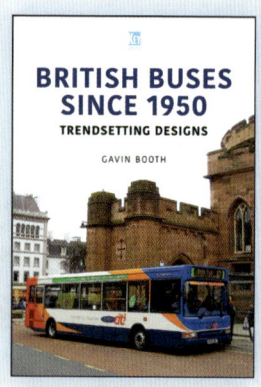

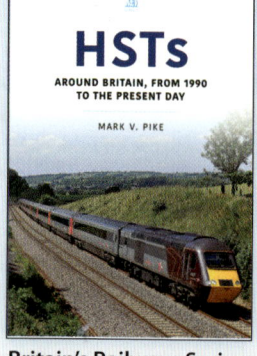